The Loathsome Burdens of the Independent Jackasses!

(A New Approach for Solving our Massive Problems!)

By
The Dictator — Adolf Hitler, Junior!

Book 051

(A Photo of a Military Barracks — P-6020)

Copyright Dedication and Introduction

By
The Leader / Führer — Adolf Hitler, himself!

ISBN-13: 978-1533470720
ISBN-10: 1533470723

00-01 [_] This not-so-funny book is Copyrighted 2016 AD, by Adolf Hitler, Junior — the Unhappy Son of Adolf Hitler, himself, who always wanted to write more books, other than *Mein Kampf,* which means *My Struggle,* which was first published during July of 1925, in Germany, which was first published in English on the 13th of October, 1933, after it was abridged / updated, which contained 720 pages, which was an autobiography of myself, Adolf Hitler, which became the most published and sold book of the time, just after the *Holy Bible,* whereby I gained a considerable amount of wealth; but, not nearly enough to finance the *Third Reich,* much less the *Fourth Great Empire,* which my Son, Adolf Hitler, Junior, will Manage with a Capital M: because he is most Qualified with a Capital Q, by Reason of the Fact that he has the most Reasonable Solutions for the World's Massive Problems, which can easily be Proven in a Courtroom with Law and Order, with a Righteous Judge in Charge of it with a Capital C, having Total Control of the News Media: because the Masses of People will DEMAND it of him, once they have Learned what he has to say, which is a very Powerful Message, and much more Powerful than *the Sermon on the Mount* by Jesus Christ, which, I must Confess is a very Good Sermon for Spiritual Children and Baby Christians; but, it Sorely Lacks any Realistic Solutions for the World's Massive Problems, whereby an Obedient Society of Intelligent People might Govern themselves with True Prosperity with a Capital T and P.

00-02 [_] All Rights are Reserved. No Portion of this Inspired Book shall be Reproduced by any Means for Sale without Written Permission from the Author, who is Adolf Hitler, Junior, which, of course, is just another Pen Name: beCause his Real Name must be kept a Top Secret: beCause his Life would naturally be in Great Danger, as you might well Imagine — that is, if your Imagination has not gone the way of World War 2, which has already been Forgotten by many Old People, and certainly has not been Experienced by any Young People. However, a few Young People can Relate with all such Hateful Wars, and especially if they have been in them. Yes, you must Remember that I was in World War 1, when it was Popular to GAS the Enemies: beCause of Satanic Inventions, which I was Strongly Against from Day one, and am still very much Against going to War for any Reason: beCause it is Possible and most Practical to Resolve our Differences Peacefully, in Courtrooms, with Righteous Judges in Charge, who keep the Courts in Order. Indeed, you may not Believe me, even as millions of Ignorant People do not; but, I made many Attempts to call the Leaders of the Nations together for a Great Meeting of the Most Intelligent Minds before World War 2 broke out; but, France, England, and America were not Interested in any such Meetings: beCause they Knew for a Fact that they were on the Losing Side of the Arguments, which were all in Favor of the Germans, who had been Reduced to TAX SLAVES of the Lowest Kind, who were Obligated by the so-called *"Versailles Peace Treaty"* to make Reparations for the Great World War that we had been in, whereby Germany was supposedly in Debt to France and England by some 4 Trillion Dollars, in Today's Money, which was an Impossible Debt for us to Repay, and especially for the German Children to Repay, who had no Part in that War, nor in any other Hateful Wars — that is, unless they were Reincarnated in the Bodies of German Children, which I Believe was and still is a Possibility: beCause, in my Sincere Beliefs, Life and Death is one Great Eternal Round, whereby each Living Spirit of each Dead Person is Judged by the Almighty God, and is thus Assigned to a New Body, whereby it can Learn the most Practical Lessons, and especially Spiritual Lessons, until it is brought to Perfection for either Good or Evil — yes, until such a Spirit is Glorified in the Holy Kingdom of All that is GOOD, or Defamed in the Unholy Kingdom of All that is EVIL, whose Head Master is Satan, the Devil, whom God Created to TEST our Spirits for their Goodness, which you do not have to Accept as the Gospel Truth; but, it can be Proven to be True in a Courtroom: beCause some People, including myself, just Happen to Remember Parts of our Past Lives.

00-03 [_] Therefore, it is Wise to be *Meek,* or Open-minded and Teachable: beCause there are many History Lessons to be Learned, which are not all Contained in that *Holy Bible,* which contains many Jewish Fairy Tales and Silly Contradictions, which can also be Proven in a Courtroom, beginning in the Beginning, in *Genesis,* when the Gods said: *"Let US make Mankind in OUR Image,"* and then goes on in *the Book of Isaiah* to Declare Emphatically that there is only ONE God, and that is JEHOVAH God, who must have Forgotten who he was talking with in *Genesis 1:26.* Yes, even a 12-year-old Child can easily Understand that something is Terribly WRong in that *Holy Bible,* which would not be Able to Stand Up in a Courtroom of any Kind, even if it were Conducted by Teenage Children, whose Minds have not been Perverted by the Outlandish Lies of RED Jews. (See *Isaiah 45:5 and 18,* plus related Verses for the Proof. See the *Blue Letter Bible* on the Internet, which contains several Versions to Study, which do not all Agree, which, itself, is a Confession that they are all WRong to some Degree.)

00-04 [_] Yes, I must point out the Fact that there are Basically 2 Kinds of Jews, who are also Identified in the *Bible,* whom I and my Son shall forever Refer to as Lying RED Jews and Honest WHITE Jews, being Represented by the Ancient Scribes and Pharisees and their Betrayer of Trust called Judas Iscariot, who Betrayed Jesus with a Kiss, if you Recall, even as Bernie Madoff Betrayed his fellow Jews in New York City, and Robbed them of tens of Billions of Dollars, who is now Resting Quietly in some Lovely American Prison, who would have to Confess in a Courtroom that he was no Honest White Jew, like Jesus Christ and his Beloved Disciples, whose Inspired Words of Provable Truths are still being Studied by Wise Intelligent Well-Educated People, Worldwide, including myself: beCause the Pure Truth is the SAME, both Yesterday, Today, and Forever, which cannot be Proven to be WRong by any Means, or else it would not be the Pure Truth! Therefore, it is Wise of us to Accept whatever Truths can be Proven, even if the whole World should happen to Disagree with us: beCause, in the End, all of the Truths will be Justified.

00-05 [_] For Example, I Discovered an Outlandish Red Jew LIE in the Holocaust Museum, in the District of Criminals, in Washington, which was written on a Placard, stating that 4 or 5 Bodies were put into just one Crematory Oven every 10 Minutes, which I Instinctively Knew for a "Fact" could not be True: beCause it would Require no less than one Hour, just to Heat Up the Oven, once a Body is put into it: beCause it Requires something like 2204 °C (4,000 °F), just to Burn Up such a Body, and no less than 2 Hours at that Temperature for an Adult Body, and sometimes as much as 4 or more Hours, which any Crematorium Technician will freely Confess in any Courtroom — that is, unless he or she is another Lying Red Jew. Therefore, do not Accept just one Person's Testimony concerning any Important Issue; but, get your Facts Straight, and get them from Honest People who Know what they are Speaking of, who are not Afraid to Swear to God that they will tell the Whole Truth to the best of their Limited Nolij.

00-06 [_] O Adolf, if what you have written is True, it Means that we cannot Trust our own United States Federal Government, which has put its "Stamp of Approval" on the Holocaust Museum in Washington, District of High-ranking Criminals, which Museum contains more than one Red Jew Lie, which should be Proven in a Courtroom, and Corrected by some Righteous Juj. Yes, it should be Proven at **"The Great Worldwide TELEVISED Court HEARING!" (That Great Meeting of the Most Intelligent Minds!)**, Book 041, whereby that Important Issue can be Laid to Rest, along with WHO Assassinated former President John F. Kennedy, WHO carried out the Oklahoma City Bombing of the Murrah Federal Building, during April 19th, 1995; plus, WHO Organized and Orchestrated the Evil Events of September 11th, 2001, which thousands of Honest Architects and Engineers Agree was a Federal Government Conspiracy with Lying Red Jews in Charge. {See www.AE911TRUTH.org for the Proof. (See YouTube Videos for *"Experts Speak Out,"* which will Enlighten your Mind more than a little bit about the Undercover Untrustworthy Cover-up WICKED Federal Government of the Divided States of United Lies!) Yes, they even Vainly Imagine that they got by with it; but, little do they Know that Master Mark Revolutionary Twain, Junior, is fixing to bring them to COURT!}

00-07 [_] And WHO is Master Mark Revolutionary Twain, Junior?

00-08 [_] Well, I was Thinking that you might Know him, seeing that he was another Gestapo SS Agent, who was Reincarnated, who also Claims to be the Reincarnation of King Solomon, himself, if you can Believe it! Indeed, I cannot Believe it — at least I could not Believe it, until I "red" **"Thu Nq MAGNUFIID Verzhun uv Thu PROVERBZ uv KING SOLUMUN in Plaan Ingglish!" (The Understandable Version of the Famous Proverbs of King Solomon in Plain English!)**, Book 028, which Bucked me clean Out of my Traditional "Saddle," you might say, and Caused me to THINK! Yes, I was about to write Master Twain OFF, as being just another Intellectual NUT, until I made up my Mind that it was not Riit to Juj any Subject, until after Lerning ALL of the Evidence, even if the Words seemed to be Mis-speld! After all, if "Nolij" must be spelled "K-N-O-W-L-E-D-G-E," why not spell "Truth" like this: "K-T-R-W-OO-T-H-E," and "Love" like this: "K-L-OUGH-V-EHE? Indeed, there are more than a dozen different ways to spell the single Sound of "OO," as in Sch**oo**l, r**u**le, d**o**, sh**oe**, thr**ough**, tr**ue**, cr**ew**, t**wo**, l**ieu**, S**iou**x, rh**u**barb, rh**eu**matism, rendezv**ous**, gh**ou**l, and p**ooh**, which could be spelled like this: Skql, rql, dq, shq, thrq, trq, krq, tq, lq, Sq, rqbrrb, rqmutizm, rondaavq, gql, and pq, which would save a lot of Space on Paper when printing all such words, and even save the Innocent Children from many Wasted Years in **"The Public School of IGNERUNT FQLZ!" (HOW we have been GRAATLEE DISEEVD!)**, Book 024.

00-09 [_] So, after Carefully Studying all of those Books, did you Learn WHO Assassinated President Kennedy?

00-10 [_] No Sir, I was still left in the Darkness of Ignorance with Poor Huck Finn and Nigger Jim, as Master Twain would say: beCause there is only ONE Way to Discover the WHOLE Truth, and that is to LEARN ALL of the EVIDENCES, which must be Presented to all of the

People in the whole World, in all Major Languages at the same Time, by Means of ONE International Television Network, just to Minimize Confusion, Cameras, and Reporters.

00-11 [_] Are you Suggesting that all other TV Channels should be SHUT OFF: so that if People Want to Watch TV, they will be FORCED to Watch **The International Television Network of The New RIGHTEOUS One-World GovernMINT (TITN of TNROWGMT)**, which would Present that Great Meeting of the Most Intelligent Minds in all Major Languages, except Latin and Hebrew, now that we are Able to Do that?

00-12 [_] Yes, Adolf, that is Exactly what I am saying. After all, I am the Reincarnation of your Chief Propagandist Minister, Joseph Goebbels, if you can Believe it, which many People will no doubt Think is just a JOKE, even as they will Assume that all of this so-called "uninspired book" is nothing but a Comedy. However, when they Discover that we are Heating Up those Crematory Ovens, once again, they will come to Accept it as a very SERIOUS Subject, which should be Addressed in that Courtroom, which is mentioned in Verse 00-06, which is the Greatest Idea since the Invention of the Light Bulb. Yes, it will be a little too Late by then: beCause the Proverbial Horses will have Escaped from the Burning Barn, you might say, and the Silver-plated Pitcher will be Broken at the Bottomless Well of Deep Understanding.

00-13 [_] And just HOW will we Know for a Fact that you are not Lying to us? Indeed, HOW can we Trust you, now that you have Confessed to being my Chief Propagandist?

00-14 [_] Well, just as soon as you Discover some Outlandish LIE that I have told in this Inspired Book, you have my Permission to put this Book in the TRASH CAN, along with that *Unholy Mutilated Bible, the Book of Mormon, the Koran,* and a Host of other Religious Lies. {See www.Amazon.com for: **"The New MAGNIFIED Version of The Book of MOORMUN!" (The Story of the White and Dark Indians in the Americas!)**, Book 040, which Debunks the whole Moronic Pack of Lies!}

00-15 [_] Well, as of now, I must Confess that I have not Heard any Outlandish Lies; but, you can well Believe that those Lying Red Jews will begin to Invent Stories about you and me, and even Claim that I am Worse than Adolf Hitler, himself, when, in Fact, I am HIM! Yes, I have already said that I am the Reincarnation of Adolf Hitler, himself, which could not be any Plainer to Understand than that. However, being the Reincarnation of him, does not make me the same Person, even though I have nothing to be Ashamed of: beCause Adolf Hitler was Actually one of the most Righteous Men who ever Lived, if I must say so, just to Inform the Younger Generation about the FACTS, which can be and should be and must be Proven in a Courtroom! Yes, if I was so BAD, Years Ago, I could have never Persuaded tens of millions of Educated People to Believe in me, and so much so as to be Willing and Ready to DIE for me — NOT beCause of being some Madman, as those Lying Red Jews LOUDLY Proclaim; but, beCause of having the Sword of Truths on my Side, which can be Discovered by Studying my Public Speeches, which are NOT Anti-Semitic, as they Vainly Imagine: beCause I am an Honest White Jew, myself! Yes, I Freely Confess it, and without being Water Boarded, nor Tortured in any Way: beCause it is nothing to be Ashamed of. After all, Jesus Christ and his Beloved Disciples were also White Jews, you might say, who, except for Jesus, were Born and Lived in Galilee, which Means that they were of the Tribes of ISRAEL, who were Separated from the Tribes of Judah, Benjamin, and Levi since Ancient Times: beCause God Preserved them for Good Reasons.

00-16 [_] For Example, the Tribe of Dan was White Blond-haired Blue-eyed People, who finally Settled in DANMARK, which the English Perverts call DENMARK: because they do not even Recognize the Fact that DAN was the Chief Warrior, and a Forefather of Alexander the Great of Greece, which can be and should be and must be Proven at: **"The Great Worldwide TELEVISED Court HEARING!"** Book 041. Yes, the Queen of Englaland is presently Sitting on the Throne of King David, himself: beCause the Coronation Stone was the Headstone of Jacob, himself, who used it as a Pillow during the Night that he Saw a Vision of a Ladder or Staircase reaching Up into the Sky in *Genesis 28,* and the Holy Angels were Descending and Ascending on the Staircase with their Golden Harps and other Musical Instruments in their Hands, who were Proclaiming in Songs the Good News about the Future Kingdom of the Gods on the Earth, which Inspired the Children of Israel to take up that Stone and Fasten 2 Flexible / Movable Rings on the Ends of it, whereby they could Carry the Stone with them by Using a long Pole, which ran through those 2 Rings, which Stone of Scone was used for Crowning all of the Kings of Israel from King David on down to the Time that the Stone was taken by Jeremiah to Scotland, from where it was taken to England and Ireland: beCause it is a Sacred Stone, upon which my own Son shall be Coronated as the KING of Kings, and the RULER of Rulers, says the Most High God! †§‡

00-17 [_] And what are the Symbols (†§‡) Representing?

00-18 [_] Well, all of those Important Things are already Explained in other Good Books, which Wise People will Discover: beCause they are Diligent Investigators, who may one Glad Day get to Reign with Jesus Christ in his Holy Kingdom, in: **"The Great World TEMPLE of PEACE!" (The Glory of Jerusalem Arises Again!)**, Book 017.

00-19 [_] O Adolf, you have me Greatly Confused. Are you saying that Adolf Hitler, JUNIOR, will be Elected to be the KING of Kings, in Jerusalem? Is that what **"The CONSTITUTION for the New RIGHTEOUS One-World GovernMINT"** states? Book 016.

00-20 [_] NO — it does not state any such Silly Thing: beCause no one would Believe it. However, among all of the Words of Confusion, God is Revealing the Truth of it, if you have the Patience to Learn it, even in his Strange Way of Revealing it, whereby many Minds can be Changed, and many Souls Converted. After all, you must always Remember that such Books are Inspired by GOD! Yes, by the same God who Inspired the *Holy Bible,* which is *"the pure word of the living God,"* according to X-amount of Preachers and Sunday School Teachers, which seems to be a little Ridiculous, if you Think about it: beCause there are more than just ONE Word, if the entire *Bible* is made up of the Pure Words of the Living God, which those Lying Preachers do not even Capitalize: beCause they have not Studied: **"Justifications for Capitalizations!" (WHY Master Twain Defies the School of Fools by Capitalizing Love and Hate!)**, Book 049.

00-21 [_] O Adolf, I must Confess one Thing, if nothing else, and that is the Fact that you have a Considerable Amount of Curious Nolij in your Head, which has Sparked an Eternal Flame within my Soul, whereby I Sincerely Want to Learn the WHOLE Truth about all such Important Subjects, including the Truth about the Shroud of Turin, which has always been a Hot Topic among Serious Scholars. After all, the very Face on that Shroud is most Tantalizing to my Spiritual Taste Buds: beCause it does Appear to be the Real Face of Jesus Christ, who must have been a very Rugged Tough Person, just to Endure the Tortures of the Stake that he was Hanged on, whereby his Hands were Crossed over his Head, and one Iron Nail was driven through the Bases of both Hands at the same Time, with just one Blow of the Roman Hammer, while 2 other Nails were driven through the Heels of his Feet to each Side of the Stake or Pole, after his Knees were somewhat Bent, whereby he could Rest his Weight on his Heels, while he got his Breath: beCause it was a Suffocating Position to be in, while Hanging there Stark Naked with Great Shame for everyone to See. Yes, it would have been much more than any of us NAZIS could have Tolerated, except for perhaps you, O Adolf, who Won the German Iron Cross for your Bravery, at which Time one of your Testicles was Shot Off; but, it did not Stop you from Preaching the Truth to the Masses of People, who are still Hungering for it, who would like to Learn just HOW you would Solve the World's Massive Problems, if you were here, Today?

00-22 [_] Trust me, I am here, Today; and I will most likely be here Tomorrow: because my Work is not yet Finished, nor will it be Finished until the Second Coming of Jesus Christ.

00-23 [_] O Adolf Hitler, we have Heard Evil Reports about thee. Are you Sure with a Capital S that you have all of your Marbles? Are you Sure that you are not a Quarter of a Bubble Off of Center? Are you Sure that you and/or your Son, Adolf Hitler, Junior, are not both CRAZY?

00-24 [_] Trust me, if I were Crazy, I could not Construct such an Inspired Book as this, and neither could anyone else: beCause it is the Work of a Genius, who is my Son — yes, my Real Son, who had to take upon himself a False Name: because of the Great Persecutions that would Naturally be Heaped upon him, if People Knew that he was Actually my Son. Yes, those same Silly People Vainly Imagine that I am the single most Evil Person who ever Lived, being the Incarnation of Satan, himself, even though it can easily be Proven that they Belong to the Synagogue of Satan, which you can read about in *Revelation 2:9 and 3:9,* which is no Lie.

00-25 [_] O Adolf, I do Hope to God that you are not Lying to us. After all, if what you say is True, we will have to Reconstruct those Crematory Ovens in Auschwitz, Poland, just to get Justice with a Capital J: beCause there is hardly any Sin in this World that is so Great as Spreading False Reports about Innocent People, such as yourself, who had no Control over the Bombing of the Railroads in Germany, whereby the Food Supply Lines were CUT OFF, which Caused Multitudes of Prisoners in Concentration Camps to STARVE — Thanks to the Wicked Allies, who have not Confessed it until this very Day: beCause they do not Want to Accept any BLAME for Causing the so-called "Holocaust," which the Lying Red Jews Greatly Exaggerated for the Sake of getting Attention, Sympathy, and BILLIONS of Dollars, which they are still Collecting from Germans, among others. Yes, they have Sold Countless Books, Videos, DVD's, Movies, Propaganda, and Memorabilia in the Name of TRUTH, while not Answering ANY of the Important Questions within this Inspired Book — such as Exactly HOW World Trade Center (WTC) Tower 7 came Crashing Down in the Form of DUST at 5:20 P.M., during September 11th, 2001, when it was not Struck by any Airplanes? Indeed, 283 Hardened Steel Columns (many of which were 22-inches by 52-inches by 47-stories tall) came Crashing Down in UNISON, like Ballet Dancers, in less than 7 Seconds, which is Physically Impossibility without the Use of EXPLOSIVES! Therefore, those Lying Red Jews are Obviously in some Secret Agreement with the Federal Government: beCause WTC Tower 7 was the Chief Headquarters for many Major Banks, plus the Central Unintelligent Agencies (CIA), the Federal Burden of Investigation (FBI), the Bureau of Alcoholics Tobacco and Firearms Fanatics (BATF), as well as

Insurance Agencies; and all of those WTC Buildings were under the Snoopervision of President George Warmonger Bush's own Brother, who was the Chief Security Guard! Strangely enough, the Vital Information was Destroyed in WTC Tower 7, which was IMPLODED that Afternoon, in Order to get RID of the Evidence! However, if anyone Doubts it, just DEMAND **that Great Meeting of the Most Intelligent Minds,** and we will Discover the Truth of it. Yes, we will Discover the WHOLE Truth, which will make the HoloHOAX Pale in Comparison, along with the MOON HOAX, which you can Learn all about on YouTube Videos. *Seek and Find.*

The Fascinating Menu for a Feast of Pure Entertainment!

— Chapter 01 —

Why would Adolf Hitler, Junior, Expose himself in such a Book?

01-01 [_] Well, first of all, I am getting Sick and Tired of Hearing Ignorant People Maligning my Father's Good Name, as if he were some Major Criminal — such as that WICKED Joseph Stalin of Russia, who had some 40 to 50 Million White Christian Russians put to Death during his Reign of Terror, which was a Major Reason WHY my Father, Adolf Hitler, wanted to get RID of him: beCause he knew about his Murders, which Grieved him. But, to make Matters Worse, the British and American Governments JOINED Forces with that Murderous Son of Satan, and Supported him during World War 2, which was a Major Crime, itself: beCause they should have Joined the Germans, and Removed Stalin from Power, which they would have Done, if they had been half so Righteous as my Father; but, they Envied the Germans for their Great Prosperity. After all, it was during the Great Depression when the Germans were Richer than any other Nation in the World — Thanks to Adolf Hitler and the National Socialist German Workers' Party, which had ZERO Unemployment and Good Wages for everyone! Yes, Germans were never Happier in all of their History, than during the late 1930's. Moreover, Adolf rode around Germany in an OPEN Car, without any Security Guards for many Years: beCause the People LOVED him. (NOTE: American Presidents have 5,000 or more Security Guards, and do not Dare to ride around in Open Cars: beCause of having so many Enemies, who would Love to Assassinate them, and Justly so: beCause they are Lying Hypocrites, who make Promises that they cannot Keep: beCause they are only PUPPETS on the Strings of Rich Red Jews!)

01-02 [_] O Adolf, if what you say is True, how come American History Books do not say so? How come *Wikipedia* does not Agree with you about the HoloHOAX and MoonHOAX?

01-03 [_] Well, it was Confessed on the History Channel, who are not altogether Liars, like those HoloHOAX Museum People are, who are Chief Liars. Indeed, the History Channel is more Professional, even though it is also in the Business of Covering Up a LOT of History, which you can Discover on the Internet, if you are of a Mind to do so, and are not Seeking to Justify the Evil Deeds of the Divided States of United Lies, some of which were Exposed in the Light of Truths by Howard Zinn, who was an Honest White Jew, who wrote a good book, called: **"A People's History of the United States,"** which goes all of the way back to the Beginning of American History, when that WICKED Christopher Columbus (1451—1506) Capitalized on the Poor Indians, and had some 20,000+ Indians Murdered by one Means or another for the Sake of Obtaining Gold, which is quite a Story for Innocent Children to Study in Public Schools, if you could Find his Book in even one of them! {NOTE: You can Discover Howard's book for FREE on the Internet, if you Search for it, just to get the Record Straight in your own Mind. After all, no Educated Honest Person Denies that the United States had a Terrible "Christian" Beginning: beCause of *"the Love of Money,"* which is the Root Cause for almost all Evils on this Earth, even as the Apostle Paul explained in *First Timothy 6,* almost 2,000 Years Ago. You can read the

New MAGNIFIED Version of it, in: **"For the Love of Money!" (The Strange Things that People Say and Do to Get more Money!),** Book 003.}

01-04 [_] O Adolf, why would an All-American Cowboy like you be Badmouthing the United States of America, which is the Best Nation on the Earth, which holds World Records for its Goodness? For Example, we have 5 percent of the Population in this World, and 25% of the Worlds Prisoners. Moreover, we hold World Records for Wasting Money on Drugs, both Legal and Illegal, and TRILLIONS of Dollars-worth per Year: beCause we have more Drug Addicts than all other Nations, combined! Indeed, we have been Imitating the Wild Mountain Sheeps and Goats, who have also been Consuming Capitalist Drugs. †§‡§§ Furthermore, we have more Rapes, more Pregnant Teenagers, more Unwed Mothers, more Suicides, more Insane Politicians, more Murderous Soldiers, more Traffic Deaths, more Gun Violence, more Murders, more Thieves, more Robbers, more Sick and Diseased People, more Hospitals, more Medical Doctors, more Money Wasted on Insurance, more Heating and Cooling Bills, more Taxes, and you Name it: beCause we are Obviously Ignorant FOOLS! {See www.Amazon.com for: **"Are Americans the Most STUPID People who ever Lived?" (HOW Working People can PROSPER and Live in PEACE Under the Rulership of a RIGHTEOUS KING!),** Book 047.}

01-05 [_] Well, in spite of all of our Evils, there are still lots of Good Americans, who would even Sacrifice their Lives to make War with me Against the Evil Empire, if I should Ask them to; but, I have Zero Interest in going to War — except to go to War with the Sword of TRUTHS, which, I dare say (and with Profound Satisfaction), is on my Side in all Cases: beCause all Truths seem to Agree with me. Indeed, I have no Quarrel with any Truth, whatever it might be: beCause I am Open-minded, and also Willing and Able to CHANGE my Mind, if anyone can Prove me to be WRong about something that I Sincerely Believe — such as the False Flag Operation of September 11th, 2001, which was "Obviously an Inside Government Job," as the thousands of Architects and Engineers of www.AE911TRUTH.org say in no Uncertain Words: beCause Military-grade Thermite was used to bring down all 3 WTC Towers, as well as Microwave Energy, according to Dr. Judy Wood, who is a very Studious Intelligent Person of a Higher Rank than most Scientists, in my Honest Opinion, who saw many Important Things that were Overlooked by NIST (National Institute of Standards and Technologies), which was working Hand-in-Hand with the *American Society of Civil Engineers,* the *American Institute of Steel Construction,* the *American Concrete Institute,* the *National Fire Protection Association,* and the *Society of Fire Protection Engineers,* as well as FEMA (Federal Emergency Management Agency) — all of whom are Guilty of TREASON, and will be Held Accountable when I am Elected to be the KING of Kings, and the RULER of Rulers! Yes, the Honest People in the whole World will VOTE for ME to be their Righteous King: beCause I am the one and only Person who has Reasonable Solutions for our Massive Problems. Moreover, I Challenge anyone to Prove me to be WRong about that, and I also Offer a ONE-MILLION-DOLLAR REWARD to anyone who can Prove my Solutions to be WRong or Unworkable!

01-06 [_] O Adolf Hitler, Junior, have you not taken far too much on yourself, and also made a Grave Mistake by using your Father's Infamous Name? Indeed, I would be too Ashamed to Admit that I am Related with him, at all, if I were you.

01-07 [_] Well, I had to get everyone's Attention, somehow, and I Calculated that the Best Way for me to Do that was to Identify myself with "the most Evil Person who ever Lived," as one of those Lying Red Jews called my Father, and with nothing to Substantiate his False Claims. After all, it was Wartime in Germany, during World War 2, which called for Drastic Measures, including those Concentration Camps, even as Hateful as they were: beCause it was the Zionist Red Jews who were Operating them! Yes, I Bet that you did not Know that little Fact of Life, huh? But, you can Discover it on the Internet, if you Search for it. Indeed, the Red Jews never did like the Honest White Jews; and therefore, they Attempted to Round Up all of them, and make little Slaves of them in Concentration Camps, which Adolf Hitler went along with: beCause he really had no Choice, if he Sincerely Wanted to Win the War: beCause that Required that he should have the Support of Lying Red Jew Bankers in New Yuck City, Lungdung, England, and elsewhere, who Supported both Sides of the War: beCause it is Financially Profitable to do so, which you might find Difficult to Believe; but, you only have to Listen to *Eustace Mullins* and other Well-Educated People on the Internet, to Discover the WHOLE Truth of it, whatever it might be — since I have no Real Idea just Exactly what it might be; but, I am Sure that the Whole Truth can be Discovered, IF we, the Tax Slaves, Interest Slaves, Insurance Slaves, Drug Slaves, and Work Slaves DEMAND **"The Great Worldwide TELEVISED Court HEARING,"** Book 041, which might Prove to be a Bit Em-bare-assing to Certain Lying Red Jews; but, they will get Over it: beCause, just for Confessing the Whole Truth, I want to Reward them with Swanky PALACES! Yes, you are Welcome to read about those Swanky Palaces in: **"The Environmentalists' Paradise!" (HOW almost Everyone could be Living in a Beautiful Manmade Paradise!)**, Book 035.

01-08 [_] I Swear to God, O Adolf, that I have never Heard of anything so Ridiculous! Why would you Reward those Lying Red Jews with anything other than 40 Lashes with a Whip, if they do not Confess all of their Sins, and especially how they Created the Bursting Housing Bubble, and set up everything for themselves to Gain no less than 10 Trillion Dollars from the American Tax Slaves, Interest Slaves, Insurance Slaves, Drug Slaves, Sex Slaves, and Work Slaves, many of whom are so Ignorant that they do not even know WHO Caused the Bursting Housing Bubble; but, you can well Believe that it was NOT the Beloved Disciples of Jesus Christ, who would have Long Ago FORGIVEN all of our Debts, if they had been the Bankers: beCause Jesus said, *"Forgive, and you shall be Forgiven."* — The Sermon on the Mount. Indeed, those Lying Red Jew Banksters claim that we Tax Slaves OWE THEM 20 Trillion Dollars for our National Debts, which they could simply FORGIVE and FORGET, if they had the Natures of Saints Peter, James, John, and Paul, who said to not Hold any Grudges. Therefore, given the Fact that those Chief Bankers freely Confess that they are JEWS, it is about Time for them to ACT like True Jews, and just FORGIVE us of ALL of our Debts, Worldwide! †§‡

01-09 [_] Well, I would Think that they would be Worthy of at least SOME Compensation for all of the Hard Work that they did to Loan to us those Trillions of Phony Dollars, and especially for all of the Money that was Wasted on those All-American Wooden / Plastic Firetrap Mouse-infested Cockroach Dens, which they call "HOMES," which no one with Clean Nostrils could Tolerate to Walk into, let alone Live in such Stinking Holes with Rats, Mice, Cats, Dogs, and even Pigs and Skunks with Highly-perfumed Buttockses, who Smell like WHORES, to me.

01-10 [_] O Adolf, do you Dare to Offend all of the Ladies, who might use Perfumes on their Butts, and Paints on their Faces? Indeed, if you make Enemies of them, you will never be Elected by any of them — at least NOT by me! Moreover, I have Checked the above Box [_] with an X: because I will Stand by my Statement, even if you Haul me up to Court. †§‡

11

01-11 [_] Well, I am not at all Worried about Obtaining the Votes of Stinking Painted Skunks, Poisonous Snakes, Porcupine Lawyers, Stinging Scorpions, Political Rabbits, Thieving Raccoons, Worm-eating Armadillos, Sneaky Opossums, nor any other Low-life Scumbags: beCause my Message is only Addressed to Honest Hardworking Reliable Trustworthy People with Common Sense and Good Understanding, who are like Workhorses, Racehorses, Saddle Horses, Milk Cows, Sheeps, Goats, Camels, Giraffes, Elephants, Wildebeests, Buffaloes, Bisons, Deers, Antelopes, Elks, Mooses, Caribous, Yaks, Musk Oxens, Reindeers, Kudus, Oryxes, Monkeys, Apes, and all Kinds of Clean Birds, who may be only one in a thousand who has been Enlightened, as of this Date; but, when God is on a Person's Side, he cannot Lose. Yes, it is just that Simple.

01-12 [_] O Adolf Junior, are you saying that Almighty GOD is on YOUR Side? If so, why was he/she/it not on your Father's Side during World War 2? Yes, WHY did he not Win the War?

— Chapter 02 —

WHY did Adolf Hitler not Win World War 2?

02-01 [_] Well, most of the Odds were Stacked Up Against him, you might say. For Example, the Axis Powers (Germany, Italy, and Japan) had about 5% of the Natural Resources in the World to Work with, while the Allies (the Communists, Socialists and Capitalists, Worldwide) had the remaining 90%, except for Unknown Oil and Gas Reserves in Ocean Beds, etc. Therefore, what could a Small Nation like German or Japan do against such Powerful Forces as the Hordes of China, India, Russia, Great Britain, and the United States of America? ‡

02-02 [_] It was a Misjudgment on the Part of Adolf Hitler to Imagine that he could Conquer the Communist and Capitalist Worlds. Therefore, he should not have Declared War on them.

02-03 [_] He did not Declare War, until after he was Provoked into it; and Honest Historians Agree with me about that. After all, the Polacks had been Attacking Eastern Germans for no less than 8 Years, before Adolf went to War against them, and Conquered them within a few Days, and only Caused the Deaths of a few thousand Fools who Resisted him, whereas George Warmonger Bush, Incorporated, Caused the Deaths, Woundings, and Displacements of MILLIONS of Innocent People, just by Attacking Afghanistan and Iraq, who had NOT Attacked America, nor even Killed so much as ONE American during the History of Iraq! Therefore, George Disobeyed his own Constitution, which he Swore to Uphold, by making a Preemptive Attack on Iraq, under the Assumption that Saddam Hussein had Weapons of Mass Destruction, which he did NOT have, much less any Capability of Delivering any such Weapons, since he did not have an Air Force, Navy, nor even much of an Army, which was Defeated in a few Days in Kuwait by George Senior, who had more Common Sense than George Junior, who was Obviously a PUPPET President. However, even George Senior Cooked up Lies about Kuwait: because it is "a Family of Red Jew Liars, who Adopted their False Beliefs," you might say.

02-04 [_] So, are you saying that Adolf Hitler was Justified by the Sins of George Warmonger Bush, Incorporated?

02-05 [_] No, I am saying that he was Justified by the Sins of POLAND, which Nation was egged on by certain Evil People in Great Britain, who should have been brought to Court for all such Evils; and then no War would have Broken Out in Europe: beCause it was an Easy Problem to Solve, even as it was in Iraq, before any War Broke Out: beCause Saddam Hussein Invited George Bush, Junior, to have a Public Televised Debate with him, just 3 Days before he was Attacked; but, the Spiritual Coward, who was Hiding Out in the Little White Outhouse, Refused to have any such Meeting: beCause he Badly Wanted to go to War in Iraq, which can be and should be and must be Proven in a Courtroom, just to get the Record Straight. Moreover, whomever Defends such a Spiritual Coward, or even Seeks to Justify any such Wars, is Suspect of being an Anti-American: beCause all True Americans are HONEST Hardworking People, like Workhorses, Cattle, Sheeps, Goats, Elephants, Giraffes, Wildebeests, Buffaloes, and Honest Trustworthy People, while the Warmongers are like Lions, Bears, Wolves, Foxes, Coyotes, Laughing Hyenas, Jackals, Wild Dogs, and Various Kinds of CATS, who can be Purring one Minute, and ready to Scratch Out your Eyes the next Minute! Indeed, *"You shall know them by their Fruits,"* as Jesus said, which is still True, thousands of Years later. Therefore, let us Inspect some of their FRUITS — yes, the Evil Fruits of CAPITALISM, which is the Chief Culprit: beCause it is the Lust for more Money, which is the Root Cause for almost all Evils, which can be, should be, and must be Proven in a Courtroom, whereby that Evil Economic System can be Rightly DEBUNKED!

02-06 [_] O Adolf, you would surely not Attack our Sacred Cow, called Capitalism, would you? After all, those Lying Red Jew Bankers would not have Gained TRILLIONS of Dollars without the Assistance of Capitalism, which is just one of their Evil Inventions for making themselves Richer. Moreover, all Americans can Thank God for that Holy Capitalism: beCause it has made it Possible for them to Raise their Standard of Living by at least 1 Tenth of 1 Percent above the Communists — that is, IF we Disregard all of the DEBTS! After all, it is Rightly said that ALL Adult Americans now OWE an Average of 120,000+ Dollars, just for our National Debts — not Counting State Debts, County Debts, City Debts, Business Debts, and Private Debts, which no one can even Count: beCause of Private Loans. Indeed, it is no Secret that the Normal College Graduate now OWES 26,000 Dollars for College Loans, and some of them Owe no less than 100,000$! {See www.Amazon.com for: **"Are you a Jobless Graduate of the SKQL uv FQLZ?" (HOW to Get a GOUD EJUKAASHUN without Robbing the Bank!)**, Book 020.

02-07 [_] Well, speaking of Debts, and Money in general, it is a Good Idea to Study what went on, Prior to World War 2, right here in the Divided States of United Lies. First of all, **"The Public School of IGNERUNT FQLZ"** did not Mention the Fact that just before Americans got into World War 2, "there was NO MONEY for doing ANYTHING," according to my own Grandparents, who Lost their 25,000-acre Farm to the Greedy Red Jew Banksters: beCause of not being Able to Pay Off the Last Payment on a Loan, whereby they had to Abandon the Farm, and leave with whatever they had in a Truck. Therefore, one might well Ask, "HOW come there was no Money for Doing ANYTHING?" Well, that was beCause those Poor Red Jew Bankers had gotten Americans into the Great Depression, just by Withholding any Money from them; but, behold, just as soon as Franklin D. Roosevelt Declared WAR, within just one Week there was an Unlimited Amount of GOOD MONEY! Yes, it had been in those Red Jew Banks all along, just like it Presently IS! Therefore, like a Magician, those Red Jew Banksters pulled out BILLIONS of Dollars from their Banks for Building Millions of Airplanes, Army Tanks, Trucks, Jeeps, Boats, Ships, Aircraft Carriers, Guns, Rifles, Grenades, Bombs, and all Kinds of Military Equipment, Uniforms, Mess Kits, Medical Supplies, Tents, Cots, Sleeping Bags, and everything that was Needed for going to WAR: beCause there is always Plenty of Money for going to War, even while hundreds of Millions of Poor People are STARVING to Death! †§‡

02-08 [_] O Adolf, are you Attempting to lay the Blame for all such Hateful Wars at the Feets of Lying Red Jew Bankers, or what??

02-09 [_] Well, without a LOT of Money, no such Wars would be Possible, would they? Therefore, there is always Plenty of Money for going to War: beCause it is an Extremely Profitable BUSINESS — yes, a Capitalist BUSINESS, we must Confess, whereby the Military Industrial Congressional Bankers' Complex has gotten very RICH! Yes, they Scammed the Tax Slaves for no less than 4 Trillion Dollars on the Recent Wars in the Middle East, and all for the Sake of so-called "National Defense," and "National Security," which also left thousands of Young Americans with the Inheritances of little Holes in Cemeteries, inside of Cheap Pine Boxes, which were equally as Glorious as the Coffins in France, Germany, Italy, Japan, China, and wherever Capitalism Thrived: beCause it is (soon *was*) an EVIL Economic System, whereby a few Rich Hogs get most of the Wealth, while the Masses of Tax Slaves, Interest Slaves, Insurance Slaves, and Work Slaves get whatever Crumbs fall from the Rich Man's Table in *Luke 16:19—31,* which is well Worth your Time to Study: beCause, not much has Changed for Poor People during the past 2,000+ Years, ever since those Lying Red Jews have been in Charge of the Great False Economy, which is Symbolized by Multitudes of Capitalist Businesses, which Appear to be Prosperous on the Outsides, and especially on the Front Sides of those Businesses; but, when you take a Good Look at the BACKSIDES of them, you Discover that it is all a Great CHARADE or Pretense of Prosperity, which is Confirmed by an Honest Study of their Financial Affairs, whereby most of them are in DEBT, and Working on the Second or Third Mortgage! Indeed, very few Americans Actually OWN their own Houses: beCause they are Mortgaged to the Red Jew Banksters, who also Own most of the Cars, Vans, Trucks, Buses, Trains, Airplanes, and all such Abominations, which STINK to the Highest Heaven, you might say: beCause of their POLLUTION, which is anything but HOLY!

02-10 [_] Surely, O Adolf, you would not be Against our HOLY CARS and other Sacred Vehicles? Would you have us to go Back to the Stone-head Age, or what??

— Chapter 03 —

The Great False Transportation Systems!

03-01 [_] O Adolf, this is where you and I are likely to Part Company, "if'n ye speeks Eevoul uv miin Krr," as Nigger Jim might say.

03-02 [_] Trust me, the American Association of Drunken Drivers has already Spoken Evil of those Unholy Dangerous Polluting Cars, along with a hundred or more other Associations and Organizations: beCause they are Truly some of the Most VILE Inventions of Greedy Men, which you will have to Agree with by the Time you Finish Reading this Chapter, or even a few Verses: beCause the Sword of Truths is on my Side, which can be Proven in a Courtroom.

03-03 [_] First of all, more than 10 Million People have been Murdered by those Dangerous Cars, Vans, Buses, Trucks, Tractors, and especially the Victims of Capitalism who have been Riding on Motorcycles, whereby there are about 4,000 Deaths on them for every single Death in an Airplane. Nevertheless, everyone who has been Watching Evening Snooze Reports, during the past 60 Years, as I have been, must Confess that Airplanes are NOT very Safe: beCause there have been tens of thousands of Deaths and Injuries in them. Therefore, an Innocent Person might Ask: "Just Exactly what is the Best Means of Transportation, since Walking is almost as Dangerous as Riding a Motorcycle?"

03-04 [_] Well, Walking is only Dangerous beCAUSE of getting Run Over by those "Holy" Vehicles that few People want to Sacrifice on the Altar of Reason and Logic. Indeed, without Cars, Vans, Buses, Trucks, Motorcycles, and all such Vehicles, very few People would Die from Walking to Work, and especially if their Work were at HOME, or near Home, where it could be and should be and will be when Jesus Christ Governs this World of Wonders: beCause there are many Great Advantages for doing it that Way, which is GOD'S Way, even as he Demonstrated in the Garden of Eden Plan, which we can Imitate, and perhaps Live as long as Adam and Eve.

03-05 [_] O Adolf, I would not Want to Live for 930 Years with all of my Aches and Pains; and I am only 50 Years Old. Indeed, I have to Consume X-amount of Drugs, just to Relieve myself of the Pains. Therefore, I am most Thankful that George Warmonger Bush, Incorporated, went to War in Afghanistan: beCause the Taliban had almost Wiped Out the Heroin Trade, by Destroying the Poppy Plants; but, now their Fields are Flourishing, once again, with the Blessings of Heaven and Earth! Yes, even God is Smiling on his Beautiful Poppy Plants. And as for those Heroin Addicts, they can all go straight to Hell, where they Belong: beCause they are Children of the Devil, who do not Deserve to Live! Moreover, you are CRAZY! †§‡§§

03-06 [_] And I was Thinking that you must be Crazy. However, it is Obvious that you are only being very Sarcastic, which is fine with me: beCause it Helps to get the Point across to the Readers, who will Understand your Ridiculous Statements, if they just read them 2 or 3 Times, I Think. Indeed, there is no Guarantee of it.

03-07 [_] O Adolf, if you Hate Cars and Airplanes so much, you must also Hate those Stinking Polluting Steel Mills and Coal-powered ElecTrickery Plants in China, India, Korea, Russia and wherever, huh? Therefore, HOW could we Transport ourselves, according to your New neo-Nazi FASCIST Economy?

03-08 [_] Well, first of all, you must Try to Understand that I am NOT a neo-Nazi, Communist, Fascist, Socialist, nor even a Dimwitcrat, Reprobate, nor Independent Jackass. Moreover, you must also Try to Understand that my Father, Adolf Hitler, had Plans for Building Beautiful Planned City States, which use Wind-powered Electric Elevators, Escalators, and Electric Subway Trains for Transportation, only: beCause the Cities are Designed for LIVING — not for making Rich Red Jew Bankers Richer; but, for Living in PEACE with True Prosperity! Indeed, each City State will Govern itself, according to its own Elected Laws and Flexible Rules, whereby Like-minded People can Live Together in Perfect Peace: beCause the Sheep-like People will not be Forced to Live with the Lion-like People, as they are right now. Therefore, it will not be a Fascist Economy at all, which was only Necessary at the Time of World War 2: beCause it Required such an Economic System to Defeat the Communists and Capitalists. However, I will be the First to Confess that no such War was ever Needed: beCause the Leaders of the Nations could have all gotten Together with my Father, and Studied the Plans for those New Cities, whereby they would have Realized that those Cities have no less than 5,000 Good Reasons and Great Advantages for Building them and Living within the Borders of them! Yes, Master Twain has many of those Great Advantages Listed in his Inspired Books, if you Want to get your Mind ENLIGHTENED! {See www.Amazon.com for: **"The Low Court of Supreme Injustices is Brought to Trial!" (Master Twain Butts Heads with the United States Supreme Court, with or without their Black Robes of Hypocrisies and Lies!)**, Book 011, plus: **"The Right Design for Living!" (A List of Great Advantages for Building Beautiful Planned City States!)**, Book 012, plus: **"Poverty Hunger Riots Strikes Brutalities Election Deceptions and Civil Wars!" (The High Price that we Earthlings have Paid for Leaving the Good Land!)**, Book 014, plus: **"Seven Great Armies of Working Soldiers!" (HOW to Provide a Way for Everyone to WORK: so as to Eliminate Poverty, Crimes, Drug Abuses, Prisons and Unnecessary Taxes!)**, Book 015, plus: **"The CONSTITUTION for the New RIGHTEOUS One-World GovernMINT!" (HOW all Peoples can get True Justice, and Celebrate the Great Year of JUBILEE!)**, Book 016, plus: **"The Great World TEMPLE of PEACE!" (The Glory of Jerusalem Arises Again!)**, Book 017, plus: **"GLORIOUS Swanky Hotels Castles and Fortresses!" (Beautiful Planned City States for WISE Intelligent Well-Educated People with Common Senses and Good Understanding!)**, Book 019, plus: **"Are you a Jobless Graduate of the SKQL uv FQLZ?" (HOW to get a GOUD EJUKAASHUN without Robbing the Bank!)**, Book 020, plus: **"The LUSCIOUS All-Mineral Organic Method of Gardening!" (HOW to Grow DELICIOUS Satisfying Foods for Potential Kingz and Kweenz in Swanky PALACES!)**, Book 021, plus: **"Did God or Satan Ordain Medical Doctors??" (Ask Huck Finn and/or Nigger Jim: because neither Tom Sawyer nor Judge Thatcher would Know!)**, Book 022, plus: **"God Speaks and the Whole World Listens!" (Fire on the Mountain from the Burning Bush by the Spirit of Truth!)**, Book 026, plus: **"Does a Good Soldier have to be a MURDERER?" (Seven Great Swanky Armies of Voluntary Working Soldiers!)**, Book 027, plus: **"Thu Nq MAGNUFIID Verzhun uv Thu PROVERBZ uv KING SOLUMUN in Plaan Ingglish!" (The Understandable Version of the Famous Proverbs of King Solomon in Plain English!)**, Book 028, plus: **"A Sure Cure for GUN VIOLENCE!" (HOW TO STOP GANG WARS and Criminal SHOOTINGS!)**, Book 031, plus: **"AIIRMWVC and Reasonable Solutions!" (Aliens, Illegal Immigrants, Refugees, Migrant Workers and other Victims of Capitalism!)**, Book 032, plus: **"Mark Twain Races for the PRESIDENCY!" (The 2016 Presidential Candidates Desperately Need Some STRONG Undefeatable COMPETITION!)**, Book 033, plus: **"ECCLESIASTES UNCOVERED!" (The New MAGNIFIED Version of Ecclesiastes and the Song of Solomon in Plain English!)**, Book 034, plus: **"The Environmentalists' Paradise!" (HOW almost Everyone could be Living in a Beautiful Manmade Paradise!)**, Book 035, plus: **"The Seven Basic Spiritual Building Blocks of LIFE!" (Faith Hope Trust Love Patience Persistence and Obedience!)**, Book 036, plus: **"DIETS!" (A Reasonable Solution for the "Eternal Controversy"!)**, Book 037, plus: **"The Nature of CAPITALISM!" (A List of the EVILS of CAPITALISM!)**, Book 038, plus: **"SWANGKEENOMIKS Rules the Roost!" (HOW all People can Prosper in a RIIT WAA, and STOP Polluting the Earth with Capitalist TRASH!)**, Book 039, plus: **"The New MAGNIFIED Version of The Book of MOORMUN!" (The Story of the White and Dark Indians in the Americas!)**, Book 040, plus: **"The Great Worldwide TELEVISED Court HEARING!" (That Great Meeting of the Most Intelligent Minds!)**, Book 041, plus: **"The Secret City of the Great King!" (HOW the True Church will Escape from the Great Tribulation!)**, Book 042, plus: **"Terrorists Beware that your Days are Numbered!" (HOW to Bring those Terrorist Attacks to a Screeching HALT!)**, Book 043, plus: **"HOW to Become a HOLY Man!" (40 Good Reasons WHY People Should FAST and PRAY!)**, Book 045, plus: **"The Proper RULES for FASTING!" (The Complete Instruction Manual for True Repentance!)**, Book 046, plus: **"Are Americans the Most STUPID People who ever Lived?" (HOW Working People can PROSPER and Live in PEACE Under the Rulership of a RIGHTEOUS KING!)**, Book 047, plus: **"An Amazing Collection of Wit and Wisdom!" (The Marvelous Tale of the Colorful Peacock from Angel Ridge, and the Strong Rope of Hope!)**, Book 048, plus: **"Justifications for Capitalizations!" (WHY Master Twain Defies the School of Fools by Capitalizing Love and Hate!)**, Book 049, plus: **"The END of CONFUSION!" (The Great CELEBRATION of the Magnificent Wedding of the Humble Honest Nations, and the Great Year of JUBILEE!) By Master Mark Revolutionary Twain, Junior!** Book 050.}

03-09 [_] O Adolf, that is a Wall of Words that is far too Thick to Bore my way through it, and far too Tall to Climb Over it, and far too Wide to go around it, and far too Deep to Dig Under it. Indeed, there is no Way on God's Blue, Green, Gray, White, Brown Earth that I am ever going to get around to Reading all such Books, even if they are the Best Books in the World: beCause I have to Earn a LIVING, which Requires that I get myself Up at 5 a.m., fix my Breakfast, Eat, Shower, Dry Off, Dress, and get ready to Drive to Work, which takes no less than 2 Hours of Fighting with the Traffic; and then, after Work, I have to Drive back Home, fix Supper for the Family, and finally get to Bed by 10 p.m., just to Repeat the same Boring Routine for 50 or so Weeks per Year, just to Pay all of the Endless BILLS that Adam and Eve Skipped Out on. However, I get to Watch all of the Evening News Reports about all of the Wonderful Tornados, Hurricanes, Floods, Fires, Mudslides, Earthquakes, Tsunamis, and other Natural Disasters: because I have a DVR, which Automatically Records it all for me, along with the latest Murders, Drive-by Shootings, Mass Murders, School Shootings, Terrorist Attacks, WARS, and all such Wonderful Exciting Things, whereby I have the Greatest Peace of Mind that you can Imagine — that is, IF you can even Relate with it, being a Cowboy from Montaner? †§‡§§

03-10 [ ] Well, to be Perfectly Honest with you, I cannot Relate with your Torments: beCause I was Born in the Bull Mountains of Montana, where I was Imprinted on Horses, Cattle, Deers, Sheeps, Goats, Pigs, Rabbits, Chickens, Ducks, Pheasants, and all Kinds of Wild Creatures, including those Snakes, Skunks, Foxes, Coyotes, Bears, and whatever. A Mountain Lion passed in front of me, one Time, going in Leaps and Bounds of about 20 feet at a Time, when I was just 10 Years of Age, which put the Spooks into me, whereby I Arrived at the House a quarter of a Mile away with just one Deep Breath: beCause the Adrenalines, or Epinephrines went Surging through my whole Body in a Second or 2, whereby I took on *"Wings of Great Faith,"* you might say, and ran over a Big Hill as if it were nothing more than a Mole Hill — Thanks to the Great God of Marvelous Creations. Yes, I Believe that I could have picked up a Car, if I had Thought of it: beCause I Felt so STRONG; and, for Sure, that Montana Mountain Lion can Thank God that he or she did not come into Direct Contact with me, or else I might have Broke his/her Neck! Yes, I Think it was King David who did something like that, if I Remember Correctly. (Please Forgive me for not wasting some Time to look it up for you. After all, it could have been a Bear who got his Neck Broke in that Story, which is all one and same thing, anyway: because David was just a Boy, who did that before he Killed Goliath, if you can Believe it. Perhaps he Hit the Bear with a Stone from his Sling. Whatever the Case, it was rather Heroic of him, I would say.) However, I am much more Concerned as to WHY you would put up with such a Boring Life of Torment as you have Obviously put up with in some Noisy Workplace? Did it never cross your Mind that there might be a Better Way to Live, without making a Capitalist SLAVE of yourself?

— Chapter 04 —

American SLAVES

04-01 [ ] For Example, my Brother and his Family worked on a little 40-acre Farm from Daylight to Dark, 6 Days per Week, for many Years, just to Feed themselves and to Sell enough Produce for buying Shoes and Clothes and Gas for an old dumpy Pickup Truck, which was a Fix Or Repair Daily (FORD) Vehicle, which "Ate Up" any extra Money that might have been Saved for all such "Emergencies": beCause of Living too far away from Inconvenient Towns. Yes, they did get by: beCause of so much Hard Work, while most of their Naaberz had to leave their Lands, and go to Work in Fragrant Dusty Chicken Houses and Capitalist Hog "Factories."

04-02 [ ] One of those Naaber Families spent no less than 300,000$ on Transportation during 40 Years, according to their own Testimony, and Stashed their Used Vehicles in the Backyard, while Hoping that another Major War might break out, at which Time they might Sell those Junk Cars for more than 100$, each; but, it never Happened, and even if it had Happened, it would not have Covered even one-hundredth of the Expenses of their Transportation. Therefore, it can be Concluded that they were General American SLAVES — as in Tax Slaves, Insurance Slaves, Interest Slaves, Drug Slaves and Work Slaves, which is True for most Americans, who actually Believe in "the American Dream," which is to Own a House, a Car, some nice Clothing, a large Flat-screen TV, and all of the "Conveniences" that might be found in a Normal American House, whereby they have "Endless Bills" to be Paid, and also consider themselves to be "Lucky," to be Able to do so: beCause Billions of Poor People are NOT so "Lucky."

04-03 [_] In Fact, one would not have to Look very far away in the Divided States of United Lies, just to Discover someone who is in a far Worse Condition, who is perhaps Sleeping in some Old Rusty Used Vehicle: beCause of not even having a Wooden / Plastic Firetrap Mouse-infested Cockroach Den to live in, much less the Money for Paying all of those "Endless Bills." Indeed, you have likely Noticed all such People, and especially if you have done some Travelling, as I have, and much more than most People: because I Enjoy Looking at National Parks, Ancient Pyramids, Artistic Churches, Castles, Fortresses, and Beautiful Hotels — including the Trump Tower in Manhattan, NYC, which has some Marvelous Marble in the Lobby, which everyone should get to See, in Person: beCause it will Inspire them to Believe in a Great Creator God, who alone could make something so BEAUTIFUL! Be Sure to check out the Chrysler Building and the Empire State Building on the way by, as well as the Grand Central Railway Station.

04-04 [_] O Adolf, I was not Aware that you are so Human, who can even Appreciate Colorful Marbles, Granites, Onyxes, and other Fascinating Stones — such as Agates, Diamonds, Rubies, Pearls, Sapphires, Emeralds, Malachite, and Gold Trimmings in Cathedrals and Theaters. Yes, I was not Aware that you could Appreciate the Good Things in Life — such as Sunrises, Sunsets, Waterfalls, Waves of Water beating against the Shores, Mountains, Lakes, Rivers, Trees, Flowers, Animals and all such Natural Things: beCause many Professing "Christians" have little or no Appreciation at all for such Things: beCause they Sincerely Believe that they are going to some Imaginary "Heaven," when they Die, and thus they will leave this World far Behind them. However, if you are the Reincarnation of Adolf Hitler, himself, I Believe that it would be Appropriate for you to be run through a large Meat Grinder, feet first! After all, when you were your Father, you brought about a LOT of Unnecessary Suffering on Humanity, which Requires some Compensation for JUSTICE. Yes, you should at least be Tormented in some Nazi Prison Camp for no less than 60 Million Years, just for Murdering 6 Million Honest White Jews! †§‡

04-05 [_] Well, it seems like you must have Skipped Over some very Important Information in Previous Chapters. First of all, my "Father" was not Responsible for the Evildoings of the Allies, who were Determined to make Fools of themselves, who "Wrote their own History" by their own Thoughtless Evil Deeds — such as Bombing the Railroad Tracks, Bridges, and Warehouses, whereby the Food Distribution was Interrupted beyond my Ability, or anyone else's Ability, to Instantly Fix it.

04-06 [_] So, Adolf, if that was the Case, which I Believe it was, WHY did you not just Surrender to the Allies, and Submit to Tax Slavery, Interest Slavery, and Reparation Bills in the Trillions of Dollars? After all, you surely Understood that you would eventually Lose such a War, seeing that Germany only had 5% or less of the World's Natural Resources to Work with?

04-07 [_] Well, speaking on behalf of Adolf Hitler, you must try to Understand that I had a Vision of a much Better World for everyone to Live in, which I will Present to you and to everyone else, later on, after we get a few Historical Events Straightened Out in our Minds. Yes, we must Establish a few Realistic Facts of Life in our Minds — one of which is the Fact that most Americans are Totally DECEIVED, Imagining that they are FREE, when, in Deed, they are

19

SLAVES of Various Kinds. Yes, I was Trying to Explain HOW my own Brother Wasted 40 Years of his Life: beCause he got ROBBED by Lying Red Jews, who, like my "Father," did not Personally Rob him; but, in a round about Way they Robbed him: beCause the Bankers Control the Money Supply, who Caused Millions of Americans to Lose their Properties by one Means or another, which they Labeled as "the great recession," instead of "The Great Recession" with Capital Letters, which you would Understand, if it had Happened to YOU.

04-08 [_] For Example, my Brother and I spent 30 Years Building Up our Farm, after I Joined Forces with him: beCause he asked for my Assistance, which I was Happy to do, and even did a lot more Hard Work on it, than he did, not Counting the Work that he did before I Arrived there — such as Constructing a 100,000-gallon Cistern for Water Storage: so that we might have Water during Droughts, which were Common Occurrences in that particular State of Confusion, which Normally has 3 Months of Drought during the Summer, just when the Garden especially needs LOTS of Water. Yes, you could call such a Cistern "Homeland Security," if you like: beCause that much Water can make the Difference between a Crop Failure and Real Success. In Fact, if you know much of anything about a Garden, you know that Water is a Critical Thing at just the Right Time, which can Prevent the Plants from getting Stunted during a Drought, and especially when those Plants are very Young, without Deep Root Systems. Therefore, a Good Water Supply is a Necessity of Life for anyone who Depends on the Garden for a Livelihood. Most of the Naaberz simply said, "To Hell with the Garden," if the Rains should Fail them, which gave to them a "Good Excuse" for letting the Garden grow up to Weeds, which I noticed was Happening the very first Year that I arrived at my Brother's Property. Indeed, I would say that 90% or more of those Naaberz took no Interest in Watering their Gardens at all, if the Rain Failed them: beCause, at the very Worst, they could always Sign Up for Food Stamps, which many of them did: beCause they had a "Good Excuse" for Failing Gardens. Indeed, there were a few Years when we did the same thing: beCause we had no Reliable Water Supply.

04-09 [_] O Adolf, did the Government have no Interest in Helping you Brothers to Obtain a Reliable Water Supply?

04-10 [_] Well, you could say that they had Zero Interest in even Hearing anything about it: beCause none of them had ever Done any such Gardening, and could not Relate with the Realities of Life: beCause they were like Inexperienced Children, even though they could Understand what we were Saying: beCause they were not Totally Stupid, if you know what I Mean; but, as with most Necessities of Life, they were not the least Interested in Providing any Way for us to Truly Prosper on the Land, even as they should be Interested: because, if every Garden is Productive, everyone will just Naturally Prosper more beCause of it.

04-11 [_] For Example, if our Garden is full of Foods to Eat, and the Pantry is full of Canned Foods, we do not have to Burden YOU, nor any other Tax Slave, to Pay for any Food Stamps for us: beCause we are Self-reliant, which is a GOOD Thing, which can easily be Proven in a Courtroom, if anyone Doubts it. Therefore, just Pretend that you are the Judge, yourself, and take that Subject into the "Courtroom" of your own Mind, and THINK about it, and you will Naturally Render a Positive Verdict in Favor of what I am Teaching to you. Yes, neither the WICKED Federal Government, nor any State Governments, have any Plans for Guaranteeing Successful All-Mineral Organic Gardens, like we were Attempting to Grow: beCause that is not within the Bounds of their Vision of "National Security," which seems to be their Primary

Concern, which Occupies most of their Governmental Conversations. However, beCause of the Urgings of the Naaberz, the Local Government finally did Install a Water Pipe, and Begged us to Connect with it; but, we Refused: beCause we had a Creek that ran with Fresh Clean Water for about 9 Months of the Year, while their Piped-in Water was Chlorinated, which we Judged was not Fit for Watering anything in the Garden, much less Drinking it: beCause, if Chlorine makes People Unhealthy and thus Unhappy, or even Insane, it could also make Animals and Plants Unhealthy, and thus Unhappy. In Fact, it has been Proven that Chlorine is POISON, which is WHY it Kills Bacterias, and also does Harmful Things to People and Animals, which can be and should be and must be Proven in a Courtroom that has some Authority to Change Things. †§‡

04-12 [_] For Example, a Righteous Judge could Order the County, State, or Federal Government to Assist People like us to Develop our own Springs of Water, and Build large Ceramic-lined Cisterns for Water Storage, just as long as we are Committed to do such Gardening, according to: **"The LUSCIOUS All-Mineral Organic Method of Gardening!" (HOW to Grow DELICIOUS Satisfying Foods for Potential Kingz and Kweenz in Swanky PALACES!)**, Book 021, just in Case there might be a Direct or Indirect Connection between Cancers and other Diseases and the Foods that we Consume, which could be and should be NATURAL: beCause, for Example, my Grandfather knew of only ONE Person during his Life who Died with Cancer; but, nowadays, one in 5 Die with Cancer of some Kind, which is likely to Increase as Time goes by: beCause more and more Children are Eating GARBAGE Foods, which the Human Body was not Designed to Consume. Therefore, all such Foods Cause Endless Ailments, which People and Animals did not used to have, which is BAD News. ‡

04-13 [_] O Adolf, a Person has to Die somehow. Therefore, what Difference does it make HOW we Die? Indeed, it has been Reported a Billion Times that you Committed SUICIDE in a German Bunker, in Berlin, which I have always Doubted: beCause the History Channel does not even Agree with that Red Jew Lie. Indeed, the Russians supposedly collected your Remains, after you were Cremated with Diesel Fuel, and took your Remains to Moscow for Safe Keeping, and for Evidence that you Shot yourself, etc. However, the DNA does not pan out, as they say, much less many other Details — such as your Teeth and Testicles, which you can Discover on the Internet, if you are Interested. Moreover, some of those YouTube Videos proclaim that you Escaped to Argentina, and Lived for many more Years, which is a Likely Thing to have Happened: beCause you were once in the British Secret Service, yourself, whereby you Learned English, as well as other Important Things that made it Possible for you to become the Person that you became — even as if some God were behind it all! In Fact, without a lot of Things Coordinating Together at the same Time, World War 2 would not have Ended the Way it did, with the Red Jews Winning it, who are otherwise known as Zionists. Yes, they Wanted to Own Palestine, which was Accomplished, in spite of all other Things Happening. Indeed, that was their Objective, which was Accomplished in 1948; but, not for the Good Health nor Happiness of the Palestinians, who now Claim that Zionists have no Right to set Claims on their Land — no more than the British had a Right to Claim America, and thus Steal it from the Indians by one Means or another: beCause they Imagined themselves to be the Descendants of the Israelites, themselves! Therefore, they were Conquering the World in the Name of their Imaginary God, who most Certainly did NOT Command them to Murder most of the Indians, whom they Imagined were Canaanites, Hittites, Hivites, Gerguziits, and Jebuuziits, etc., etc. †§‡

04-14 [_] Well, there is some Old Saying about the Spoils going to the Victors. Therefore, in their Way of Thinking, whomever Conquered whomever had all Rights to Claim for themselves, including the Negro Slaves, which were Stolen by Zionist Jews from Africa, which they had already been doing for Centuries. Indeed, they were the "Secret" Shipmasters, which you do not read about in American History Books, which should be Revised and Updated every few Years, according to whatever Truths are Discovered and Proven in a Courtroom: so as to get the Record Straight for all of the Children, who might not Like to become Future Tax Slaves, who Owe Enormous Debts to those Lying Red Jews. ‡

04-15 [_] For Example, the Federal Government of the Divided States of United Lies, Proudly Proclaims that Americans Owe no less than 20 Trillion Dollars for the National Debt, alone; but, they never do say WHO they Owe the Debt to: beCause, if the Masses of People Understood that they Owe the Money to Lying Conniving Red JEWS, they might Think Twice before Packing their Bags and going SOUTH, to Venezuela, Brazil, Argentina, or even to Mexico: beCause Life is Actually much Better in any one of those Countries, if a Person has a little Money: beCause those Countries have the Great Advantage of FREE Heating and Cooling — at least at the Right Elevations, which could Save a Family no less than 5,000$ per Year — that is, if one should presently Happen to be Living in some not-so-Paradisacal Place as New England, or Chicago, where one might find a very Small Apartment for 1,500$ per Month, for Rent, which does not even have a Garden to Feed oneself from, much less a 100,000-gallon Cistern for "Homeland Security." ‡

04-16 [_] O Adolf, not everyone is Enticed to Own a Garden of any Kind, even if the Space is Free: beCause they just Naturally HATE Gardening, and especially when the Weeds are 14 feet Tall, with Roots 6 feet Deep, and covered with Sharp Thorns: beCause it is a Hateful Place to Work in.

04-17 [_] Well, if you are so Stupid as to not Keep those Weeds Under Control, by being a Good Master, it is Understandable WHY you would Imagine that Gardening might be a Hateful Occupation, when it is Actually one of the most Pleasant and Self-rewarding Occupation in the World: beCause of all of the Delicious Fruits and Vegetables that one can Grow in such a Garden, which is WHY that I made Gardening MANDATORY Schooling when I was in Control of Things in Germany, which was also a Good Thing: beCause we did not have X-amount of Drug Addicts in Germany at that Time, as you Americans now have, who Reject Truths without a Justified Cause, who actually Imagine that Gardening might be a BAD Thing for Children to Learn, when it is, in Fact, one of the most Rewarding, and also Draws Children Closer to God: beCause Natural Laws must be Followed, just to be Successful at it. For Example, if you Want very Tasty Kale Greens, you must Plant the Seeds during the Autumn, a Month or so before the first Frost: beCause those Frosts Greatly Improve on the Flavor of the Kale Leaves, which can be Protected a little, and Endure until Springtime, by using a few Bails of Straw or Hay around the Plants, which Straw can be pulled away during nice Sunny Weather, whereby the Kale will keep right on Growing, all Winter, if it is a Mild Winter. Otherwise, the Row of Kale can be Covered with Straw, until Springtime arrives, when that Row can be Uncovered, at which Time the Kale will keep on Growing for a Springtime Harvest.

04-18 [_] O Adolf, I can remember Growing so much Kale in a little Patch, only 4 feet Wide and 40 feet Long, that it Fed the entire Family all of the Kale that we could Eat, and had no less than

40 Baskets of Kale to give to the Salvation Army, which Served it to the Poor Victims of Capitalism, without anyone Explaining to them HOW they could Grow their own Kale by: **"The LUSCIOUS All-Mineral Organic Method of Gardening!" (HOW to Grow DELICIOUS Satisfying Foods for Potential Kingz and Kweenz in Swanky PALACES!)**, Book 021. In Fact, no one bothered to Explain to those Poor People what a Swanky PALACE IS, much less HOW they could Obtain a Place to Live in their OWN Swanky Palace! However, according to Master Twain, all of those Good Things are quite Possible and most Practical, which a Righteous One-World GovernMINT would Provide for everyone who is Willing and Able to Learn and Work, even if they were Grade-school DROPOUTS! After all, it is Possible to do as little as 30 Minutes of Work per Day, on Average, and Grow more Foods that you can Eat, if you have the Land, and are Organized by the Assistance of some Good Master, who knows his Gardening as well as a Stone Mason might know how to Build Beautiful Stone Walls.

04-19 [_] Well, if my Master Plan were Faithfully Followed, almost everyone in the World would be Living in **"GLORIOUS Swanky Hotels Castles and Fortresses!" (Beautiful Planned City States for WISE Intelligent Well-Educated People with Common Sense and Good Understanding!)**, Book 019, within only 6 Years: beCause we would go at it like going to War, which I will Explain in the next Chapters for your Enlightenment.

04-20 [_] O Adolf, did Master Twain Steal your Ideas; or, did you Steal his Ideas??

— Chapter 05 —

Seven Great Armies of Working Soldiers!

05-01 [_] Well, to Answer your Question, neither one of us Stole any of our Great Ideas from neither one, nor from anyone else: because he and I are the same Person with Different Pen Names, among others: beCause it is Necessary to keep the Federal Burden of Investigation (FBI) Off Guard, if you know what I Mean, which is a Military Diversion, you might say. After all, if I had Wasted hundreds of Billions of Dollars, Researching Solutions for our Massive Problems, without Delivering so much as ONE Reasonable Solution, I Believe that I would be Worthy of being Retired from the FBI. What do you Think?

05-02 [_] O Adolf, it is not the Duty of the FBI, nor of the Central Unintelligent Agencies (CIA), to Discover any Reasonable Solutions for any of our Problems, except for things like Terrorist Attacks. Nevertheless, God have Mercy on us, if almost all Americans become "Terrorists": beCause of being Mistreated by the Federal Government, which Needs to be Dethroned.

05-03 [_] Well, I just Happen to have a Reasonable Solution for those Terrorist Attacks, which you are Welcome to Study, in: **"Terrorists Beware that your Days are Numbered!" (HOW to Bring those Terrorist Attacks to a Screeching HALT!)**, Book 043.

05-04 [_] O Adolf, I cannot figure out WHY you Adopted such a Horrible Pen Name as "Adolf Hitler, Junior," when "Master Mark Revolutionary Twain, Junior," was Good Enough to Satisfy the Mind of almost all Readers, who have a lot of Love and Respect for Mark Twain; but, Zero Love and Respect for Adolf Hitler?

05-05 [_] Well, it is my Honest Opinion that your Judgment concerning that Subject is not Correct: beCause, even if People do not Love me, they must Respect me for my Great Accomplishments. For Example, you might not know it; but, the German Working Soldiers mixed and poured more Cubic Meters of Concrete in just 6 Months, under the Streets of Berlin, than 10 Times the Volume of the Great Pyramid in Egypt! Indeed, you should find that quite Impressive with a Capital I, since no such Massive Project, except the Interstate Highways, has ever come close to that in America, nor anywhere else in this World of Wonders, which Required True Leadership, which was only somewhat Matched by the Egyptians and Maya Indians, who Built Uxmal {Qsh-mawl}, in Mexico, which you can Study in *Wikipedia*. Actually, it is my Belief that the Egyptians did not Actually Build the Great Pyramid in Egypt: beCause it was Built by Enoch, who was of the Seventh Generation from Adam, who had the Help of Alien Giants, who were of a Superior Race of People. †§‡

05-06 [_] O Adolf, I am more Impressed by how a small Country, like Germany, nearly took over the whole World, under the Leadership of Adolf Hitler, who could not possibly be your "Father" by any Means: beCause you were Born before he Died. Therefore, you could not be the Reincarnation of Adolf Hitler, which can be Proven in a Courtroom. †§‡

05-07 [_] Well, I must Agree with you, even though I am Falsely Accused of being the Reincarnation of Adolf Hitler, which is WHY I said so, early on in this Book, just to get everyone's Attention, if Possible, with the HOPE that they would at least read a few Pages of this Inspired Book, which is the Difference between Lightning and the Lightning Bug, as Mark Twain would say: beCause Inspired Books are as Rare as Lightning, when Compared with the Hordes of Lightning Bugs, or Fireflies, which can be seen by the Billions in the United States during an Evening in June: beCause they are quite Common, who are Symbolical of those Children who Tweeter Messages to each other, while my Inspired Books are like Lightning Striking! Yes, they are Dramatic, Revolutionary, and Mind Expanding!

05-08 [_] O Adolf, Morley Safer told Brian Lamb in an Q&A program on C-SPAN, years ago, that writing a book was a "Torture," being Extremely Difficult. Therefore, I am wondering if the same thing is True for YOU? Is it a Torture for you to Write a Book?

05-09 [_] No, Absolutely NOT! In Fact, if it were a Torture, I would not Bother myself to do it: beCause there are many other Kinds of Work that I Love to do — such as Stone Masonry, Tile Setting, Carpentry, Gardening, Cooking, Sewing, Plumbing, and especially Inventing New Tools, and other Inventive Things, which Explains those **"GLORIOUS Swanky Hotels Castles and Fortresses!" (Beautiful Planned City States for WISE Intelligent Well-Educated People with Common Sense and Good Understanding!)**, Book 019, which just Happen to have more than 5,000 Good Reasons and Great Advantages for Building them and Living within the Borders of them, which cannot be said for anything else on this Earth! Indeed, Wearing ROBES have at least 77 Advantages over Normal Clothing — such as the Fact that one cannot Forget to Zip Up his Pants: because of not Wearing any Pants; but, such Robes also have a few

Disadvantages — such as not being Good for Riding Horses, Climbing Telephone Poles, and being Popular among Ignorant Fools, who Vainly Imagine that Jesus Christ was some Kind of a "NUT," just for Wearing Robes and Cloaks. Trust me, Robes are so Comfortable that once you Wear one for a Week or so, you will be "Spoiled," and never be Able to Willing Return to your Vain Traditional Complicated Clothing of Suits and Ties, etc.

05-10 [_] O Adolf, I want to Learn about those **"Seven Great Armies of Working Soldiers!"** **(HOW to Provide a Way for Everyone to WORK: so as to Eliminate Poverty, Crimes, Drug Abuses, Prisons and Unnecessary Taxes!)**, Book 015, on www.Amazon.com for FREE!

— Chapter 06 —

Will Adolf Hitler, Junior, Institute the Mark of the Beast?

06-01 [_] Well, first of all, for the Sakes of those People who do not know what *"the Mark of the Beast"* is all about, I must give a short Explanation of it: because they would not otherwise Understand it. The Expression comes for *the Book of Revelation, Chapters 13—16,* in the *Bible,* which is the Last Book, otherwise known as the *Apocalypse,* which means "the complete final destruction of the world," according to the Dictionary, which is not at all Accurate: because the Earth will Endure for millions, if not billions of Years. Therefore, it would Depend on what the Definition of "World" is? Actually, in Reality, it is a Book about the End of Confusion, which is otherwise known as *Babylon* in the *Bible,* which Means "Confusion."

06-02 [_] Therefore, rather than *the Book of Revelation* being a "Negative Thing," it is Actually a "Positive Thing": because we all Long for the Glad Day when Confusion will be brought to an End, and the World will be Living in a State of Peace and Quietness, which could be in our Generation, if we so Choose. Indeed, it is all within our own Power, Collectively, if we Act on it — that is, IF we take Action to make it Happen: beCause God has given to us that Freedom: beCause of having the Liberty to Choose between Good and Evil. {See www.Amazon.com for: **"The END of CONFUSION!" (The Great CELEBRATION of the Magnificent Wedding of the Humble Honest Nations and the Grand Year of JUBILEE!)**, Book 050.}

06-03 [_] For Example, we can Willingly Choose to Build those **"GLORIOUS Swanky Hotels Castles and Fortresses!" (Beautiful Planned City States for WISE Intelligent Well-Educated People with Common Sense and Good Understanding!)**, Book 019, whereby we can Solve more than 5,000 Problems; or, we can Choose to Continue on with the same Confusion and Madness that has Preceded us, which Jesus Christ called Vain Traditions. (See *Matthew 15:3 and Mark 7:8—13.* Notice the word, *many.* See *Colossians 2:8 and First Peter 1:18.*) In other words, if you Lived on the Island of Traditional Cannibals, you would likely Believe that Eating other People is GOOD, even though it is Actually BAD: beCause you would not Want other People to be Castrating you, and Fattening you up in a Cage, to be Eating on you when you got to the Perfect "Ripeness" — that is, when your Muscles were Fully Developed; but, still Tender and Juicy, at about 18 Years of Age! (See *Wikipedia* for the Full Details.)

06-04 [_] So, the Great Question is this: **"Is the Mark of the Beast a GOOD Thing, or a BAD Thing?"** Well, I say that it is a Bad Thing: beCause it gives the Government far too much Control over the People, while Denying them of the Freedom to Sin with the *Prodigal Son of Luke 15,* whereby he came to his Right Senses: beCause of being Free to Choose his own Fate. Otherwise, he might have become a Lifelong Rebel. Therefore, we need to Build those Beautiful Planned City States, in Order to AVOID the Mark of the Beast: beCause it is not Needed in such a Good Economic System: beCause most of the People are simply Living at Home and Attending to their own Gardens and Home-craft Workshops and Sales Shops.

06-05 [_] O Adolf, I Fail to Understand the Advantages for having any *Mark of the Beast.* Perhaps you could Enlighten our Minds about that Subject?

06-06 [_] Well, with the Mark of the Beast System, all Money will be done Away with: beCause each Person will Buy and Sell his or her Goods and Services by Using his or her Personal Permanent Positive Identification Numbers — such as your Social Security Numbers — which will be found in a little Computer Chip, known as a Radio Frequency Identification Chip (RFID), which is presently Installed in Passports and Driver's Licenses, and is commonly used to Identify Pallets of Grocery Items with Universal Product Code (UPC) Numbers. Therefore, when Money is done Away with, it will also do Away with many Major and Minor Problems. For Example, ...

-01 [_] How could anyone *Rob* a Bank, Gas Station, Grocery Store, or even a single Person, if there were NO Coins nor Currency in Use? (NOTE: There are multiple millions of such Robberies each Year, Worldwide.)

-02 [_] How could anyone Trade Cash for Illegal Drugs, if there is NO Cash? Therefore, the Illegal Drug Business will come to a Screeching HALT, which will Prevent X-amount of Murders, which will Solve many Massive Problems at the same Time!

A-[_] I Agree. Mothers will be able to Sleep in Peace, knowing that their Sons are not out on the Streets trading Drugs for Money.

B-[_] Less Policemen will be needed to Patrol the Naaberhoud.

C-[_] Children will not be Overdosing on Drugs.

D-[_] Most Drug Businesses will got Out of Business.

-03 [_] How could anyone Collect Cash or Currency as Ransom Money for Kidnapping anyone, if there is no Money in Use? Therefore, Kidnapping for Ransom Money will simply Cease!

-04 [_] How could anyone Trade Goods and/or Services by Means of Black-market Businesses that Deal with Money?

-05 [_] How could anyone Hire someone to Murder someone, if they have no Money to Offer to them for the "Job"?

-06 [_] How could anyone Write a "bouncing" Check, if there are no Checks?

-07 [_] How could anyone Buy Explosives, or Materials for making Explosives, without being Detected by the "Big Brother" Government Computer Systems?

-08 [_] How could anyone Abuse Legal Drugs, or even Foods and Drinks, without being Detected by the Computers?

-09 [_] How could anyone Avoid the Census, and what Need would there be for taking a Census, since the Government would already Know ALL?

-10 [_] How could anyone Avoid Paying Income Taxes, since all Taxes would be Collected Automatically by the Computers.

-11 [_] How many "Illegal Immigrants" would there be, if no one can Buy nor Sell anything without the Government Computers knowing all about it?

-12 [_] What Need would there be for Passports, seeing that your Identification Number would be Universal, and would Work in all Nations that Accept the RFID System?

-13 [_] How many Taxes would have to be Collected for Controlling "Illegal Immigrants," seeing that all Borders and Border Guards could be Removed?

-14 [_] How could any Nation Manufacture any Weapons without the New Righteous One-World Government Officials knowing all about it: because of Knowing what Materials have been Bought and/or Sold?

-15 [_] What Need would there be for Debt Collectors, seeing that there is no Money to Loan, and no Debts to Collect: beCAUSE of Establishing a New RIGHTEOUS One-World GovernMINT, which has an Unlimited Amount of New Money, in the Form of CREDITS, which must be Earned by Honest Labor, which is Credited to your "Bank Account," which is simply your RFID Numbers in the Government Computer? (See Chapter 10 for Explanations about those CREDITS.)

-16 [_] What Need would there be for any so-called "Drug Wars," seeing that no Drugs could be Traded for Money? That alone will Save Billions of Dollars per Year.

-17 [_] How could anyone Avoid Paying Business Taxes, which might amount to a Total of 2% of the Net Income from the Sales of Goods and/or Services: beCause of having such a Small Federal Government: beCause each Planned City State would Govern itself, Tax itself, and do whatever it Voted for to itself? (NOTE: Master Twain Explains in his Good Books HOW to Avoid all Taxes, if you are Interested in True Freedom.)

-18 [_] How could anyone Fail to Pay their "Property Taxes," seeing that no one would Actually Own any Major Property — such as their Multi-Trillion-dollar Swanky Palace, which might consist of no less than a thousand Beautiful Stone Dome Home Complexes, which have Polished Marble Walls, Polished Granite Floors, Agate Windows, Waterfalls, Living Rivers of Pure Water, tens of thousands of Fruit Trees, Home-craft Workshops with Top-quality Tools to Work with, Sales Shops with Polished Marble Walls, Gymnasiums, Tennis Courts, Swimming Pools, and Huge Cisterns for Water Storage, which no one could Afford, even if they Slaved Away their Lives for 60 Years: because a Swanky PALACE would be Worth more than a thousand times whatever POOR Bill Computer Software Gates could Afford! But, everyone could Afford to do at least 3 or 4 Hours of Common Labor per Day, just to Help Build all such Palaces, and then Move into them, Tax-free, Debt-free, Loan-free, Interest-free, Insurance-free, and so on!

A-[_] I Agree, it is a very Good Plan, just as long as everyone gets to Participate, and everyone does a Good Job of whatever they do.

B-[_] I Believe that it is God's Plan, whereby everyone can have everything in Common, even as the First Church of Jesus Christ had, who Worked Together for a Common Cause. †§‡

C-[_] I Confess that it would be a Good Plan to Follow: because almost everyone in the World could end up Living in a Beautiful Swanky Palace. However, just as long as Capitalist Hogs are in Charge of the World, it will not be Done.

D-[_] Damn you, Adolf Hitler, Junior — you are Attempting to Destroy our Beloved DUMBmocracy, whereby most Americans are Totally DECEIVED, while Imagining that their Election Deceptions will Solve their Problems, if they just Vote for the Right-WRong / Rong-Riit Parties. †§‡§§

E-[_] Educated People Know that such an Idea is Revolutionary, and might even Eliminate our ElecTrickery Bills: beCause it is now Possible and most Practical to Build HUGE Swanky Electric Power Plants. †§‡ {See www.Amazon.com for: **"UNLIMITED ENERJEE 99 Percent Pollutions Free!" (HOW to Obtain FREE ElecTrickery, Worldwide!)**, Book 029.}

F-[_] I Fail to Understand what this Inspired Book is all about. Will the Fuehrer Order us to Join **"The Swanky Associations of Working Soldiers!" (A Fascinating Collection of Various Kinds of Voluntary Working Soldiers!)**, Book 018?

G-[_] God Knows that most People have now Suffered Long Enough, whereby they Agree that it is a Good Idea to Establish a GOOD One-World GovernMINT, which has an Unlimited Amount of New Money in the Form of CREDITS, which must be Earned by Honest Labor, which one can Use to Move about from one Planned City State to another, until one Discovers the one that he or she Likes Best: because of having FREE Government Transportation, Worldwide, even if Young Working Soldiers must be DRAFTED into some Swanky Army, just to get those Underground Railways Constructed, after which those Working Soldiers can Move into Swanky PALACES! Yes, that will be their Reward for Sacrificing 6 Years of their Lives.

H-[ ] To be perfectly Honest with you, O Hitler, I must Admit that it would be a Great Improvement for almost everyone, except for those Lying Red Jews, who now Live in High-rise Apartment Houses in New Yuck City, who would have to Humble themselves beyond Humiliation, just to get to Live in one of those Beautiful Swanky Palaces: beCause few of them are Willing to Work for a Living! Yes, that would be Extremely Humiliating for them; but, they would no doubt get Used to it, after a Year or 2 of Working in their own Gardens and Home-craft Workshops, which would be quite an Improvement over Communism, which did not Provide any Gardens, Well-made Tools, Spacious Workshops, Sales Shops, nor Spacious Stone Dome Home Complexes that cover an entire Acre of Land, each! {See www.Amazon.com for: **"The Right Design for Living!" (A List of Great Advantages for Building Beautiful Planned City States!)**, Book 012.}

I-[ ] I Admit that 99% of the People in this World of Woes would LOVE to Live in Swanky Palaces within those **"GLORIOUS Swanky Hotels Castles and Fortresses,"** but, NOT if they had to Sacrifice their Beloved Cars, which they Worship as Idols. Yes, the Image that Speaks has Fully Persuaded them that Life is not Worth Living, unless one OWNS such a Car, and Especially a Normal All-American Wooden / Plastic Fire-trap Mouse-infested Cockroach Den, whereby they can Continue to Pay ElecTrickery Bills, Heating and Cooling Bills, Insurance Bills, Property Taxes, and Endless Repair Bills: beCause all such Houses are Designed by the Synagogue of Satan, you might say, whereby the Ignorant People are made into Eternal SLAVES, and do not even Realize it! {See my next Book, called: **"Are We Tax Slaves of a Lower Order than Lying Red Jews?" (HOW to be Liberated from all Slavery!) By Adolf Hitler, Junior!** Book 052.}

J-[ ] Justice Demands that we, the Masses of People, DEMAND **"The Great Worldwide TELEVISED Court HEARING!" (That Great Meeting of the Most Intelligent Minds!)**, Book 041, whereby we can Discover whether or not Adolf Hitler, Junior, is our SAVIOR, or just another Radical Insane Politician?? Yes, he should be the Chief Judge in Charge of the Courtroom, which should be Held in Saint Peter's Basilica, in Rome: beCause it is the Ideal Place to Meet, being in the Shape of a Cross, whereby his Opponents can Sit at his Left Side, and his Advocates can Sit at his Right Side, and the News Reporters and Witnesses can Sit in the "Leg" or Nave of the Cross with their Laptop Computers.

K-[ ] King Jesus would NOT Permit such a Great Meeting of the Most Unintelligent Minds to Convene: beCause he Personally wants to get Rid of the Devil when he Comes in all of his Naked Glory, being about 400 feet Tall, riding a Great White Horse that is equally as Tall, being Dressed for Battle, with all of his Armor on, running on the Clouds at 5,000 Miles per Hour: so that every Eye can get to See him during One Day, when he Comes with a Great Host of Flying

29

Saucers — even Millions of them! Yes, what a Great Day that will be, when the Master Farmer Arises to SHAKE TERRIBLY the WHOLE EARTH, whereby every High Tower will FALL! Yes, King Jesus will be Extremely Happy to See the Crushed and Burned Bodies of Billions of People, and especially those hundreds of millions of Innocent Children and Little Babies! †§‡§§

L-[_] Lots of Laughs! King Jesus has no such Plans. Indeed, he does not Glory in the Destruction of his People, nor take any Pleasure in any such Vile Actions: because he is a Man of Perfect Peace, Compassion, and Harmony.

M-[_] MONEY is the Solution for all of our Massive Problems. Indeed, if we had Enough Money, we could Use it Wisely for Building those **"GLORIOUS Swanky Hotels Castes and Fortresses!"** — even if they are much more Modest than Adolf Proposes, whereby a Stone Dome Home Complex might Cover a Quarter of an Acre, rather than one whole Acre of Land, which is 210 feet by 210 feet, whereby the Roofs would be Covered with those LUSCIOUS All-Mineral Organic Gardens, Vineyards, and Orchards, which would be directly in FRONT of each Stone Dome Home Complex, instead of being in the Backyard, where most Gardens are presently Located: because they are easier to Protect with Guard Dogs. However, there will be no Need for any Guard Dogs in those Beautiful Planned City States, which are Built in Great TERRACES, which will have Stone Walls a hundred feet Tall in those Great Terraces, even though Walls 50 feet Tall would be Sufficient to Protect any such City State, even from Tidal Waves 300 feet Tall! †§‡§§

N-[_] Not everyone Wants to Live in such a Planned City State, which might be a Mile Tall, in those Great Terraces, which are Built with HUGE Cisterns, which would Naturally have those Hateful Rules and Regulations to Follow, whereby a Person would not even be Free to Spit nor Piss in his own Garden. †§‡

O-[_] Are there no OPTIONS to Choose from? Could each Planned City State not have its OWN Rules and Regulations, whereby everyone would be Free to Choose WHERE he or she Wants to Live, and with WHOM they Want to Live? For Example, I Like Dogs; but, my Husband prefers Cats. Therefore, he could Live in the Cat Fortress, while I could Live in the Dog Fortress; and thus we could both be Happy. †§‡

P-[_] All People will be Free to Choose whatever Rules and Regulations they Want. Therefore, it is just a Matter of Discovering LIKE-MINDED People to Live with, which can best be done by everyone Filling Out and Filing the SURVEYS of their VALUES, which can be Discovered in: **"LIGHTNING Versus the Lightning Bug!"** (HOW almost Everyone can become Moderately RICH without Telling Any Lies nor Selling Any Trash!), Book 001.

Q-[_] The Great Question is this: **"Will we be Wise and Use our DUMBmocracy to ELECT Adolf Hitler, Junior, to be our Righteous KING, or DICTATOR; or, will we go on Suffering for another thousand Years**

under the Dominion of those Greedy SELFISH Lying Red Jews, who Control the Money Supply, who could just Forgive us of any Debts, and do their Best to Establish a New RIGHTEOUS One-World GovernMINT, if they had their Riit Miindz?? †§‡

R-[_] Religious People do not like the Sound of a RIGHTEOUS One-World Government: beCause that Implies that such a Government might not Allow them to have Freedom to Worship God as they Please: beCause of being a Religious Government, which will just Naturally Assume that its State Religion is the One and ONLY True Religion, which might be the False Religion of Adolf Hitler, Junior, himself, who would just Naturally LOVE such Power and Control over us! Therefore, such a Wicked Government will be Persecuting all other Religions — at least until they are Converted by the Sword of Truths. †§‡§§

S-[_] Satan has you Greatly Deceived, and also Imagining Superstitious Things. After all, if there were only ONE True Religion, then all of the others would have to be WRong. Likewise, if there were any Perfect Translation of the *Bible,* then all of the other Translations would have to be wRong. Therefore, the Wise and Honest People will DEMAND: **"The Great Worldwide TELEVISED Court HEARING,"** Book 041, whereby all Religions, Sciences, and Political Parties can be Proven to be TRUE or FALSE, GOOD or EVIL, Righteous or Wicked, whereby People will be Able to Rightly Judge for themselves WHERE to Live, and with WHOM to Live. After all, we have Heard enough Lies for one Lifetime!

T-[_] I Totally Agree with that last Statement — that we have all Heard enough Lies for one Lifetime, which should be Proven to be Lies in an Open Courtroom, whereby everyone is Free to Testify in Favor of the Whole Truth, whatever it might be, even if such Truths Prove all of us to be wRong about all Subjects! †§‡

U-[_] I Understand what you are saying, and it Sounds Good to me; but, what are the Chances of People Changing their Minds, after being Brainwashed with so many Capitalist Lies for so many Years?

V-[_] Queen Victoria would DEMAND such a Great Meeting of the Most Intelligent Minds, just to Discover WHO might be RIIT! After all, it is not a Great Shame to Confess that we have been WRong about a lot of Important Subjects; but, it is a Great Shame to HIDE the Truth: beCause, only the Whole Truth can Liberate us from our Prison of Lies, and thus Liberate us from all of our SINS, which are Transgressions of the Laws of the GODS, for whom is the Kingdom, the Power, and the Glory Forever: beCause *"God"* Means, *"The Supreme Ruling Family of Holy Ones, who have been Perfected in the Furnaces of Afflictions."* Therefore, God is ALL that is GOOD, while the Devil is All that is EVIL, being the Great Deceiver, who has Deceived all of the Nations by the Abundance of his DRUGS, whereby he has most Minds DRUGGED, and so much so that they cannot even Understand such a Simple Book as this! †§‡

31

W-[_] World War 3 will Resolve all such Issues, and those Lying Red Jews will Win, once again: beCause they Control the Propaganda Machine, you might say. Yes, they Control the Information that the Masses of People get to Learn. Therefore, unless this Inspired Book is Published in all Languages to all Peoples, Worldwide, and even "Red" aloud from the Housetops, the Masses of People will go on Slaving Away their Lives: beCause of Sincerely Believing that it is GOOD to be Independent Jackasses! Yes, they Vainly Imagine that they are Free with a Capital F, even while they are Tax Slaves, Interest Slaves, Insurance Slaves, Drug Slaves, Sex Slaves, and Work Slaves! Indeed, it is a PARADOX of the Human Mind, which can only be Straightened Out by ONE Means, which is by the Sword of TRUTHS, which only Demands a Fair HEARING in an Open Court!

X-[_] X-amount of People will not Want their Favorite TV Channels SHUT OFF, just to Hear the Evidence, even if that Evidence is the Most Fascinating Information that they have ever Heard: beCause they are Addicted to their Favorite TV Channels. Moreover, others are Addicted to their Computer Nonsense, whereby they Distract their Minds from the Realities of Life, while others are Addicted to Video Games, Ball Games, Animal Worship, Sports and other Nonsense, whereby they will not be Interested in any such Great Meeting of the Most Intelligent Minds. †§‡

Y-[_] Well, that was True, just Yesterday; but, Today a New Star has Arisen, whose Light of Truth Shines Brighter than the Sunstar, itself — at least within the Mind of the Person who Studies such Good Books as he has Written. ‡

Z-[_] The ZEAL of Master Mark Revolutionary Twain, Junior, will make it all Possible, even if a so-called "TYRANT," like Adolf Hitler, must Arise again, who will be Falsely called the Anti-Christ! Yes, it is the Will of Almighty God. †§‡§§

-19 [_] How could anyone Avoid Paying Child Support Payments, since such Money would Automatically be Deducted from a Person's Bank Account, no matter where he or she might Move to, who could never Escape from his or her Responsibilities to his or her Children?

A-[_] We must Allow for the Fact that with such a Good Government System in Force, very few Divorces would Occur: beCause Potential Married Couples could use their Computer Chips Wisely with the SURVEYS of their VALUES, in Order to Discover Life-mates of Like-mindedness, and thus have Compatibility: beCause of having most Beliefs in Common with each other, as well as Potential Friends of Like-mindedness, who could all Live within the same Order of Swanky Fortresses, if they Wanted to. {NOTE: There are almost Countless Advantages for this one Advantage: beCause of the Chain-reactions of Advantages, which would be True for many Generations to come among Like-minded People, who would be ever so Thankful for Discovering other People of Like-mindedness and Compatible Persuasions. For Example, they would not have "Eternal" Arguments about which Political Party might be Best of them: beCause of already coming to an Irrefutable Agreement that ALL of them are WRong and Unnecessary, even as all False Religions are wRong and Unnecessary — except to Teach to them that one Important Lesson about Satan's Tricks, who is the Father of all Lies, including those Religious Lies — such as People going to Heaven when they Die! (See *John 3:13, King James Version [KJV]*, which could be WRong; but, it is Doubtful: beCause there is a great deal of Evidence to Prove that People go to Graves when they Die, even if their Spirits go into the Sky, where they wait around for New Bodies to be Born in, even as they have done since the Beginning of Time, several Billions of Years Ago, since all Spirits were Created in the Beginning, according to the *Scriptures,* whereupon with their Completion, the Gods RESTED for a thousand Years: beCause there was no Man as yet to Till the Ground, just as it is Recorded in *Genesis 2,* which is NOT another Creation Story; but, it is a Continuation of *Genesis 1,* which should not have been Separated by another Chapter, much less Mutilated by Lying Red Jews, who Deliberately Caused CONFUSION, which was also never Needed, except to Teach to us some Good Lessons — namely that Evil People cannot be Trusted, and that we should not put our Trust in them, even if they seem to be Authority Figures — such as George Warmonger Bush, Incorporated, whom Americans in general Trusted to make the Right Decisions in Afghanistan and Iraq, which turned out to be Political and Military Disasters — Thanks to a False Trust!

B-[_] Such a Beastly System as you Propose, O Adolf, would not Allow Teenagers to get Children Pregnant: because Condoms would be Outlawed.

C-[_] I Confess that all Fathers should Support their Children, even if they are Born outside of Holy WedLOCKS: beCause Society Demands Responsibility for all such Actions, which are easy to Control by having Ancient Greek Sex, which is Man on Man, Face to Face, and Stark Naked, until they Fight it Out, which is by Far the most Enjoyable Sex in the World, which is otherwise known as Frot Sex, which is CLEAN Sex, whereby it is Impossible to Spread AIDS and other Sexually-Transmitted Diseases (STD's) which are easy to Avoid. †§‡ {See www.Man2ManAlliance.org for the Proof.}

D-[_] The Devil would have you to Believe all such Outlandish Lies: because he is a Sodomite at Heart. God will Damn you to Hell for Frot Sex, just like he Damned those Greeks for Practicing it for 400+ Years, when they became the Hellenist Greeks, who Built the most Sophisticated Stone Buildings in the World, and set up their Greek Gods and Goddesses, whereby they made Fools of themselves! †§‡

E-[_] Educated Historians know that the Greeks had a Superior Society, with almost no Crimes, and Healthy Happy People who Lived for hundreds of Years, which is why we Accept Greek DEMON-ocracy, whereby the Masses of People have MOB Rulership. †§‡

F-[_] You Fail to Understand the Whole Truth of it. We have never Practiced Greek Democracy in the Divided States of United Lies: beCause, only the Best of Male Greeks were even Permitted to Vote in their Elections, which should also be

True of us, if we Sincerely Want to Prosper in a RIIT WAA, and Live in Peace. Yes, each Potential Elector should have to Study: **"LIGHTNING Versus the Lightning Bug!" (HOW almost Everyone can become Moderately RICH without Telling Any Lies nor Selling Any Trash!)**, Book 001, and then Fill Out and FILE the SURVEYS of their VALUES on the Internet for everyone to Study and Criticize, just to Qualify to Vote for Government Officials.

G-[_] God Knows that THAT would be the Best Plan, except that I might Lose my Freedom to SIN! †§‡

H-[_] Hold everything! Wise People Understand that not all People are the Same, nor do they Want to be the Same: beCause they Want to be Unique and Different. Therefore, each Planned City State will be Unique, having their own Elected Laws and Flexible Rules, which will be Enforced by their Elected King or Queen, whereby they can Live in Peace with each other: beCause it is not Right that People, who are like Lions and Wolves, should be Ruling Over People who are like Sheeps and Goats. Therefore, we have to Learn to be HONEST about all such Things, and give People a Chance to Live with their own Kinds of People, whereby they can be Happy and Contented.

I-[_] I am an Indian; but, I do not like Indians: beCause they are Stupid People, whose Minds seem to be Drugged most of the Time, whereby they are Living in some LSD Dream, which is not Realistic; but, it seems Good to them, even if it makes no Sense. †§‡

J-[_] Jesus Christ would NOT Separate the Sheeps from the Goats. (See *Matthew 25:32, Gay King James Version — KJV.*) †§‡

K-[_] King Jesus will most Definitely Separate the People who are Like Sheeps and Goats from the People who are like Lions and Wolves. Yes, I would Bet my Last Kilogram of Blubber on it. †§‡

L-[_] Lots of Laughs! Jesus Christ is nothing but a Jewish MYTH, which has Served its Purpose to Prove all of you Silly People to be Ignorant, Superstitious, Greedy, Selfish, and LOATHSOME in the Eyes of the Gods, who would have all People to Work Together like the Army Ants, Honey Bees, Schools of Fishes, and Birds that Flock Together as ONE: beCause those Gods LOVE the Unity of Cooperation and Harmony, which can only be Accomplished by Establishing **"Seven Great Armies of Working Soldiers!" (HOW to Provide a Way for Everyone to WORK: so as to Eliminate Poverty, Crimes, Drug Abuses, Prisons and Unnecessary Taxes!)**, Book 015, which is a Companion Book of: **"Poverty Hunger Riots Strikes Brutalities Election Deceptions and Civil Wars!" (The High Price that we Earthlings have Paid for Leaving the Good Land!)**, Book 014, which is a Companion Book of: **"The Gospel According to Saint Twain!" (The Good News from the Most Modern Perspective!)**, Book 013, which is a Companion Book of: **"The Right Design for Living!" (A List of Great Advantages for Building Beautiful Planned City States!)**, Book 012, which is a Companion Book of: **"The Low Court of Supreme Injustices is Brought to Trial!" (Master Twain Butts Heads with the United States Supreme Court, with or without their Black Robes of Hypocrisies and Lies!)**, Book 011, which is a Companion Book of: **"GOOD NEWS for REBEL WOMEN!" (HOW almost all Wives can become Moderately RICH without Leaving their Homes! Guaranteed!)**, Book 010, which is a Companion Book of: **"WHY are some Preachers so POOR?" (HOW they could almost all Get RICH!)**, Book 009, which is a Companion Book of: **"A Sound Argument for Masters and Servants!" (WHY Everyone Needs a Good Master, and every Master Needs Good Obedient Servants!)**, Book 008, which is a Companion Book of: **"The PRAYERS of PUMPKINHEADS!" (Even God Needs a Little Humor to Cheer him Up!)**, Book 007, which is a Companion Book of: **"The Washington Journal is a FARCE!" (C-SPAN Managers are not very WISE!)**, Book 006, which is a Companion Book of: **"WHY do I have to be Surrounded by CRAZY PEOPLE?" (Do almost all People Feel like they are Surrounded by Crazy People??)**, Book 005, which is a Companion Book of: **"HOW to Prepare for CLIMATE CHANGES!" (The Wisest Plan for Mankind to Follow!)**, Book 004, which is a Companion Book of: **"For the Love of Money!" (The Strange Things that People Say and Do to Get more Money!)**, Book 003, which is a Companion Book of: **"What is WRong with those Professing Christians?" (A Self-Examination of the Heart of the Body of Good Government!)**, Book 002, which is a Companion Book of: **"God Speaks and the Whole World Listens!" (Fire on the Mountain from the Burning Bush by the Spirit of Truth!)**, Book 026, which is a Companion Book of: **"Does a Good Soldier have to be a MURDERER?" (Seven Great Swanky Armies of Voluntary Working Soldiers!)**, Book 027, which is a Companion Book of: **"A Sure Cure for GUN VIOLENCE!" (HOW TO STOP GANG WARS and Criminal SHOOTINGS!)**, Book 031, which is a Companion Book of: **"AIIRMWVC and Reasonable Solutions!" (Aliens, Illegal Immigrants, Refugees, Migrant Workers and other Victims of Capitalism!)**, Book 032, which is a Companion Book of: **"Mark Twain Races for the PRESIDENCY!" (The 2016 Presidential Candidates Desperately Need Some STRONG Undefeatable COMPETITION!)**, Book 033, which is a Companion Book of: **"ECCLESIASTES UNCOVERED!" (The New MAGNIFIED Version of Ecclesiastes and the Song of Solomon in Plain English!)**, Book 034, which is a Companion Book of: **"The Environmentalists' Paradise!" (HOW almost Everyone could be Living in a Beautiful Manmade Paradise!)**, Book 035, which is a Companion Book of: **"The Seven Basic Spiritual Building Blocks of LIFE!" (Faith Hope Trust Love Patience Persistence and Obedience!)**, Book 036.

M-[ ] Do you have any Idea how much MONEY would be Required for each Adult Person in the World to Obtain a Hand-carved Leather-bound Edition of each of those Inspired Books?

N-[_] Not everyone would Want such Books; but, whomever does Want them should have them to Study for FREE on the Internet, which would be the Case, if I were the Elected King of this Mountain. †§‡

O-[_] Are there no Options? Could we not SHARE all such Hand-carved Leather-bound Books in Public LIE-braries? Sorry, I meant TRUTH-braries! †§‡

P-[_] Wise People from around the World will just Naturally be Wanting their own Private Copies of all such Inspired Books: beCause of being the Best Books in the World, in spite of any Meaningless Flaws. †‡

Q-[_] The Great Question is: **"Will such a Book as this ever FLY?"** After all, Adolf Hitler does not have a very Glamorous Reputation for being a Wise Man.

R-[_] History Revisionists will get the Record Straight, Guaranteed: beCause, if they do not, Adolf Hitler, Junior, will have them Boiled in HOT Used Motor Oil in Saint Peter's Plaza, in front of Saint Peter's Basilica, in Rome, and also Publicize it on **The International Television Network of the New RIGHTEOUS One-World GovernMINT**: so that everyone left Alive might Hear, Watch, and FEAR! †§‡

S-[_] I Seriously Doubt that such an Evil Thing will ever Happen. After all, we are NOT Barbarians of any Kind nor Color. Therefore, if you Sincerely Believe that such a Thing will Happen, please Check the above Box in Verse R, and this Box [_] with an X.

T-[_] It is now Time to Serve the World with True Justice, which can only be done by Holding that Great Meeting of the Most Intelligent Minds, and then get all of the Historical Records Straight, which will Naturally Require some Time.

U-[_] I Fail to Understand HOW we will go about Discovering those People with the Most Intelligent Minds?

V-[_] Well, Victoria, whomever has Filled Out and Filed the Complete SURVEYS of their VALUES, and Posted them on the Internet, is a Person with a Superior Mind, being of the Superior Race of People — whatever his or her Color or Race might be: beCause only very Intelligent People will have enough "Brains" to Comprehend such Surveys, which is also True of all Inspired Books, which Dimwits and Valentines cannot Understand: beCause they are Blinded by their Pride and Lusts. Yes, Ask Queen Victoria, if you Doubt it. †§‡

W-[_] Wait a Minute! Queen Victoria DIED a Long Time Ago. Therefore HOW could we Ask her anything?

X-[_] Well, X-amount of Ignorant People will be Consulting their Unholy Mutilated *Bibles,* for Reasonable Solutions, and mostly for Ways to Escape their Day of Judgment: beCause they are Sure that God would not leave them Stranded without any *Rope of Hope* to Cling to. However, if they would be so Brave as to Search the Inspired Words of Master Mark Revolutionary Twain, Junior, they would Discover a very Strong *Rope of Hope,* whereby they would not be Let Down into any Deep Dark Pit of Confusion — such as they now Find themselves in, and without any *Rope of Hope* at all! Yes, all of their so-called "education" will Fail them: beCause it is Worthless Nonsense!

Y-[_] I Yearn for the Time when Babylon comes to an END.

Z-[_] You can now Act with Zeal for the Sake of Truths, and Help it to Come to an END, just by going to Bed, come next April 21st, and Refuse to get up, until the Leaders of the Nations Cooperate with us, and thus DEMAND: **"The Great Worldwide TELEVISED Court HEARING!"** Book 041.

-20 [_] If the Mark of the Beast could Persuade most People to Move into Swanky Fortresses, that alone would be Worth it: beCause of Eliminating the Need for Automobiles, which would Greatly Cut Down on Pollution.

A-[_] I Agree — we can all Live Happily without Cars, Vans, Buses, Trucks, Tractors, Motorcycles, 4-Wheelers, Snowmobiles, Snow Blowers, Chainsaws, Weed-eaters, Lawnmowers, Garden Tillers, and all such Abominations. Indeed, Wise People never did Need any such Evil Things: because they are Inventions of Satan and Sons, Incorporated.

B-[_] I Beg your Pardon — I LOVE my Pickup Truck, which makes it Possible for me to Transport my Groceries Home, to my Farm, where I Grow Corn, which does not have a Garden to Feed me: because it is far too much Work to Grow it.

C-[_] I Confess that a Garden could be Set Up Properly for Feeding a Person; but, there are other Things that we like to Eat — such as Bacon and Eggs for Breakfast, and Imported Lobsters and Shrimps for Supper. Therefore, it is Impractical for a Farmer to Raise all of his own Foods. †§‡

D-[_] Damn it! I want my Freedom to Drive my Diesel-powered Pickup, even if it does Pollute the Air, Water and Land: because that is why God Created all such Pickup Trucks. Yes, in the Beginning, he told Adam to get himself a Pickup Truck: beCause there was no Way that he could Live a Healthy Happy Life for 930 Years without a Pickup Truck! †§‡§§

E-[_] The Garden of Eden did not Require any such Stinking Abominations. Moreover, we can make our own Gardens of Eden, if we are not Spiritual Cowards. {See www.Amazon.com for: **"The Environmentalists' Paradise!"** **(HOW almost Everyone could be Living in a Beautiful Manmade Paradise!)**, Book 035.

F-[_] I Fail to Understand HOW the Wheat and Corn would be Harvested without Tractors and Trucks? You have got to be a NUT, O Adolf!

G-[ ] God Knows that the Goats, Sheeps, Buffaloes, Deers, Antelopes, Elks, Horses, and other Beasts could take Care of the Grasses and Grains on the Great Plains, even as they did for thousands of Years before the Greedy Capitalists Sons of Satan arrived, who Murdered the Beavers for their Pelts, which Destroyed their Dams, which Destroyed whole Flocks of Birds and other Wildlife that Depended on those Dams and Ponds: beCause it was a Harmonious Well-Organized Environment for them. Therefore, if you Disagree with that, you will be CURSED: beCause Adolf will have your Ass Whipped, and sent to Work for 40 Years in a Red Jew Concentration Camp, if not in a Rock Quarry! †§‡

H-[ ] Heaven have Mercy on us — is there no other Hope for Mankind, than to get another World War going — all beCause those Lying Red Jews Refuse to Submit to the Sword of Truths, and Help Adolf to Publish his Good Books?

I-[ ] Innocent Children want nothing to do with such Hateful Wars.

J-[ ] Justice Demands that we have at least one more World War, just to Finish what Adolf Hitler Failed to Accomplish, whereby we might get RID of those Lying Red Jews, who have Known all along that they are Chief Scammers. Indeed, they need their Lights put OUT! †§‡

K-[ ] Why do you not let King Jesus put their Lights Out, if he Wants to? Why are you Determined to get Revenge on them by doing more and more EVIL, when it is Possible and most Practical to Overcome Evils by Doing GOOD Works — such as Building those **"GLORIOUS Swanky Hotels Castles and Fortresses!"** Book 019. Yes, King Jesus would LOVE it: beCause no one would have to Die for it. In Fact, the Jews — both White and Red — could Build their own Beautiful Planned City States, and Attend to their own Gardens, Vineyards, Orchards, and Home-craft Workshops, and thus Live in PEACE, even within a few Miles of those Palestinians, who could Do Likewise, if they were of a Mind to Do so, and STOP Acting like Spoiled Children. ‡

L-[ ] Lots of Laughs! Those Palestinians will be an Eternal Thorn in the Side of Israelis, unless they are Moved to Arabia, where they will have LOTS of Space, and will be Able to Build their own **"GLORIOUS Swanky Hotels Castles and Fortresses,"** even in Vast Deserts, where there is presently no Water: because it is now Possible to Transform Ocean Water into Coconut Water, by Distilling it, and Soaking Crushed Limestone in it, which will Transform it into Good Water for Coconut Trees, Mangos, Date Palms, Figs, Cantaloupes, and whatever Grows over there, which will Require a little Experimenting; but, behold, in the End, they will Wonder WHY they did not Think of it a thousand Years Ago? Indeed, with the Correct Tools to Work with, they could have all been Living in Swanky Palaces, all of this Time — at least since World War 2. ‡

M-[ ] If they had had enough MONEY to Work with, they might have Thought of it; but, being such Poor Deprived Beggars, WHO could Think of it?

N-[_] Nostradamus could have Thought of it, and probably did Think of it; but, did he Prophesy anything about those **"GLORIOUS Swanky Hotels Castles and Fortresses"** — knowing that they would Solve so many Massive Problems? NO!‡

O-[_] O Adolf, is it not Bad Enough that you should Defame your own Name with such a Ridiculous Book as this, without Defaming Nostradamus, also? In my Honest Opinion, you are still a Disgrace to Mankind: beCause Nostradamus never mentioned anything about Swanky Fortresses, much less Swanky Wages. †§‡

P-[_] People like you should do more Research, before you put your Pillow in your Mouth. Indeed, all of the Holy Prophets Prophesied about those **"GLORIOUS Swanky Hotels Castles and Fortresses"**: beCause of Understanding the Importance of them for Solving our Massive Problems, which Proves the *Holy Bible* to be TRUE. (See *the Books of Daniel and John.*) †§‡§§

Q-[_] The Great Question is this: **"Disregarding any Silly Prophecies in the Crazy Bible, and elsewhere, will enough People be Willing to EXPERIMENT with the Construction of those Swanky Fortresses, just to Discover whether or not they might be the Most Practical Way to Live, seeing that Master Twain Claims that they have more than 5,000 Good Reasons and Great Advantages for Building them and Living within the Borders of them?"** †§‡

R-[_] I Refuse to Study: **"The Right Design for Living!" (A List of Great Advantages for Building Beautiful Planned City States!)**, Book 012: beCause that Book COSTS TOO MUCH! Indeed, not even my entire Church could Afford it, whereby they might Share it, along with all other Inspired Books: beCause of having a Public TRUTH-brary in the Church, which all Churches should have. ‡

S-[_] Satan is Busy Deceiving all of you People, making you Imagine that you can Solve your Massive Problems without Consulting the Most High God, who did not Send nor Ordain Adolf Hitler, nor Mark Twain, much less their Juniors: beCause God does not Work like that: beCause it might Confound Worldly-wise People, who might be Driven Insane by it all — that is, if they have not already Lost their Sanity with Nigger Jim and Huck Finn, along with Insanity Claus, Mother Easter, who has 12 Breasts, and other Goddesses? Surely this is nothing but MADNESS, as MuhamMAD might say, just after Murdering X-amount of Innocent Victims of Religious Nonsense. †§‡§§

T-[_] Time will Prove you to be WRong. Almighty God or Satan did Send and Ordain all Important People: beCause God has Certain Lessons to Teach to Mankind — and especially to those Testosterone-filled Muslims, who have a False Testimony about MuhamMAD, who Taught Lies, who was a Murderer, Child Abuser, and whatever, which can be, should be, and must be Proven in a Courtroom. †§‡ (See *Romans 13.*)

U-[_] I Understand what you are Saying; but, I have my Doubts about it ever Happening in Reality: beCause there is not one Muslim in a thousand who would be Humble Enough to Confess that MuhamMAD was in Fact, MAD, whose Lyrics Prove it in the Unholy KORAN. For Example, it clearly states that all "Infidels" should be Destroyed, which was NOT the Way of Christ, nor of Moses, even though the *Bible* might Lead such an Ignorant Person to Believe that: beCause the Jews were supposed to Slaughter all of the People in the Land of Canaan: beCause the Hebrew "God" was not Aware of the Consequences of such an Act of Genocide, which would Ruin his own Chosen People, and give to them a Superiority Complex, whereby they might Imagine that they are the Superior Race of People, when they are no Better than the remainder of us, if not Worse. Yes, Historically, they have Proven themselves to be much Worse than other Peoples, whereby they have been Hated for Centuries, and are still Hated by such People as Adolf Hitler, Junior, who would like to Exterminate ALL of them! †§‡ (See YouTube Videos for: "World Defeated the Wrong Enemy" and "Why Hitler wasn't Evil.")

V-[_] That is simply NOT True, O Vindictive Liar: beCause I have Clearly Stated that ALL Peoples should be Assisted to Help Build those **"GLORIOUS Swanky Hotels Castles and Fortresses,"** which Naturally INCLUDES the Jews, even if they are the Worst of the Bernie Madoff and Judas Iscariot Club. After all, none of them can be Rightly Blamed for the Sins of whomever wrote that Genocidal Information in the so-called *"Holy Bible,"* which is a Mutilated book, which does not even Mention **"The Proper RULES for FASTING!" (The Complete Instruction Manual for True Repentance!)**, Book 046. ‡

W-[_] It is True that the Bible Lacks a LOT of Important Information for Overcoming the Devil; but, it Lacks no Words for Describing HOW to Build the Tabernacle, Temple, and other Nonsense — such as the Offerings, Washings, and Purifyings, which can be found in *Leviticus,* which no Modern-day Levite Observes, according to the Letter of the Law, or else those Levite Priests would have to Inspect the Private Parts of each Person who comes into the Congregation, which Excluded Women: beCause they are just Inherently Unclean Creatures, who also had no Right to Speak in the Congregation, until the Apostle Paul came along, and Commanded them to be Silent in the Churches. †§‡§§ (See *First Corinthians 14:34; Numbers 30:13, Esther 1; and Deuteronomy 23:1.*)

X-[_] X-amount of Women have long ago Cut those Pages Out of their Holy Bibles, just by Ignoring them, if nothing else. After all, People have Grown Up, Spiritually, since the Days of the Apostle Paul. †§‡

Y-[_] Yahovah God would Disagree with you.

Z-[_] Zebras would Agree that Women have Equal Rights with Men. Therefore, they have Equal Rights. Period. †§‡

-21 [_] With the Mark of the Beast System, everyone will Pay all of their Bills on Time.

-22 [_] The Mark of the Beast System will make it Impossible for Telephone Bills to not be Paid. However, all Telephones should be Free of Charge, and all Calls should also be Free of Charge to whomever Joins: **"The Swanky Associations of Working Soldiers!"** **(A Fascinating Collection of Various Kinds of Voluntary Working Soldiers!)**, Book 018.

-23 [_] All Telephone Calls will be Recorded in One-World Government Computers by the RFID. Therefore, Threats of Violence on Telephones will Cease. †‡

-24 [_] How could anyone Call C-SPAN's *Washington Journal* more than once per Month?

-25 [_] Who could Threaten anyone with Blackmail for the Purpose of Gaining Money, since there will be no more Money?

-26 [_] Who could give Unauthorized Gifts in Secret to Politicians, or to anyone else, without being Detected, and thus Taxed for it?

-27 [_] Who could cross a Border without being Detected just as soon as they Attempted to Buy something, at which Time a Red Light would Flash at the Grocery Store, and then they would be Arrested by the Security Guards?

-28 [_] Who could Steal something without being Detected, if they got Caught with some Item that was not Listed among their Goods in the One-World Government Computers, which would Operate on an Independent Closed Circuit Line, which only Government Officials would have Access to by Means of their own **Personal Permanent Positive Identification Numbers**, plus a Special Code for each Cash Register and Store, whose Clerks would be Government Workers, only, or Authorized Businesspersons, who would be Responsible for all Transactions?

-29 [_] Who could Steal a Baby from a Hospital without being Discovered, sooner or later, since each Baby would have a Computer Chip (RFID) Implanted in it, just the same as any Lamb, Kid, Puppy, Calf, or Colt?

-30 [_] Who could Buy Souls for the Purpose of making them into Prostitutes in some Foreign Country, which presently happens every Day by the hundreds, if not by the thousands or tens of thousands?

-31 [_] Who could Steal Livestock, without being Discovered, since each Cow, Horse, Hog, Dog, or whatever would have its own Personal Computer Chip?

-32 [_] Who could get by with Pouching Wild Animals, such as Rhinos, for the purpose of Selling their Horns, since there would be no Black Market Businesses?

-33 [_] Who could Buy or Sell any Kind of Slaves, Worldwide, since this System would be Used Worldwide, which would do Away with Money Exchanges, which almost everyone Hates?

-34 [_] Who could make themselves into Prostitutes for Obtaining Money without being Detected by the Computers, since there would be no Cash to Trade for Sex? Indeed, Child Pornography and Illegal Prostitution would simply Cease. However, if you Lived within a Seventh Swanky Fortress, you could still Enjoy all Kinds of Prostitutes: beCause they would be Legal, along with just about everything else that you can Imagine, including the Use of Drugs of all Kinds: beCause the Prodigal Sons should be Free to Exercise their very DUMB DUMBmocracy in their Cities. †§‡

-35 [_] What Person with a Bad Record could get onto an Airplane without being Detected, since the Life History of each Person would be within those One-World Government Computers, and no one could go anywhere without being "Watched" by those Computers and the Policemen who have Access to them?

-36 [_] Who could Transfer Money from one Country to another without being Detected, since "Money" would merely be "Credits" in the One-World Government "Banks," which everyone would have to Earn by Means of Honest Labor, including the Business Manager, who would also get to Live within a Swanky Palace, if he Wanted to? Otherwise, he or she could Live within any Normal City of Confusion, where there are NO Swanky Palaces: beCause, not even Rich People can Afford them!

-37 [_] Who could Collect Money for Jobs that were not Completed, without being Detected, even if they Moved to another State or Country? Indeed, their RFID would Follow them wherever they might go, and Reveal everything that they might Buy or Sell, including Pornography, Drugs, Drinks, Potato Chips, or whatever.

-38 [_] Who could Commit any Crime at all, without being Watched wherever they went for the Remainder of their Lives, if they were Caught?

-39 [_] Who could Pump Gas without Paying for it, since it would Require their Mark or RFID Chip in order to get the Pump to Operate?

-40 [_] Who could Sell Homegrown Fruits and/or Vegetables without being Detected, whereupon Taxes would be Collected, Automatically?

-41 [_] Who could Rent anything without being Watched / Monitored?

-42 [_] Who could Buy an Extra Pack of Beers without being Detected and Monitored?

-43 [_] Who could Buy more than 3 Small Meals per Day without being Detected, if they were Ordered to Limit or Restrict their Diets? Indeed, who could even Buy an Extra Bottle of Prune Juice for flushing out their Bowels, after Eating too much Dog Food and Hog Slop at the Death and Hell Restaurant? In Fact, who could Buy so much as a Pizza, without being Detected and Corrected, if they were too Fat, or even if they had High Blood Pressure, whose Diets could have a Restricted Amount of Salt?

-44 [_] Who could Spy on anyone in some Foreign Country, without being Detected by that RIGHTEOUS One-World Government?

-45 [_] What Government could make Illegal Weapons, without being Detected by the New RIGHTEOUS One-World Government, who would Know every Thing that is Bought and Sold: beCause each Thing would have a Special Unique NUMBER to Identify it, including Diamond Rings, which would have RFID Chips Implanted in them.

-46 [_] Who could Deny the Answers that they Checked on their own Personal SURVEYS of their Religious Spiritual Political Governmental Social Sexual Moral Business Labor and Habitual VALUES?

-47 [_] Who would Need a Passport?

-48 [_] Who could Lose their Passport?

-49 [_] Who could get their Passport Stolen?

-50 [_] Who could get their Identification Numbers Stolen, since every Body could have more than one Computer Chip Implanted within them, one of which only the Possessor of it would Know the Location of it, as well as the One-World Government?

-51 [_] Who would Need to Pack a Wallet with Countless Plastic Cards, Phony Paper Money, and so on? Just Trash it and the Contents.

-52 [_] What Old Ladies would have to Fumble around in their Purses at Check-out Counters, Searching for Ink Pens to write out and Sign Obsolete Checks, while Wasting everyone's Precious Time, who is also Standing in Long Lines during Paydays, since every Work Day would be an Automatic Payday at the End of it?

-53 [_] Who would have to Wait in a Long Line at some Grocery Store at the Check-out Counter, while someone is Searching in his or her Pocket or Purse for some Loose Change?

-54 [_] How could an Inheritance get Lost or Misplaced, and thus not even be Claimed?

-55 [_] Who could Forget their Identification Numbers, since every Body would have Computer Chips within it?

-56 [_] Who could be Misidentified at an Airport, or at any other Port or Place on Earth, even on a Private Yacht in the Middle of the Ocean of Forgetfulness?

-57 [_] Who could get the WRong Prescription Drugs?

-58 [_] Who could you get Fired from a Job for something that was the Fault of someone else, who got Misidentified?

-59 [_] There would be no more Double Bills on anything. (That is a Major Problem for Businessmen, who get Charged 2 or more Times for the same Things. For Example, I used to Buy 40 Bags of Portland Cement at a Time, direct from the Factory, and Paid

Cash for the Cement; and then, a Month or so later, I would get a Bill in the Mail for the same Cement. Therefore, if I had had a Secretary, who was not Aware of it, she could have Paid the Bill again, even 2 or 3 Times: because the Bills just kept coming. Therefore, Capitalists have to be Watched like a Hawk: beCause they are Sneaky Creatures.)

-60 [_] The Mark of the Beast will make it Impossible for Cars to be Stolen: beCause the Cars will not Start without Identifying the Drivers to be the Owners.

06-07 [_] O Adolf, if you had Learned about such a Money Game when you were the Leader of Germany, there is little Doubt that you would have been the First to Implement that System.

06-08 [_] Well, you Completely Misunderstand me. First of all, you might Imagine that I Wanted Total Control over other People, which History does not Support. For Example, when we took over France, the only Law that we Imposed on the Masses of People was a 10 p.m. Curfew, which they were Happy to Obey: because it was much Better than the Mistreatments that other Nations would have Imposed on them. For Example, when Russian Communists took over Eastern Germany, they did all Kinds of Vile Things to them, and even Built the Berlin Wall, just to keep them Locked IN, while everyone would be Free to Leave a Swanky Fortress at any Time, if they have not Committed any Crimes, for which they might be Banished from all Swanky Fortresses. Therefore, it is not a Wise Thing for anyone to Do: beCause there will be many Cities of Confusion where they can continue to Sin, if they Want to; but, no one will be Forced to Steal, Lie, Cheat, nor Murder, just to Earn a Good Living at a Swanky Fortress, which might eventually Function with as little as only 2 or 3 Hours of Work per Person, once the Fortresses are Finished.

06-09 [_] O Adolf, you Paint a Picture that is Unrealistic. First of all, you will not be Able to Persuade even one Nation to go along with your Master Plan: because most People like to OWN their OWN Possessions.

06-10 [_] Well, I do not Object to that Plan, if someone Wants to OWN his own House, Tools, Furniture, Books, Business, Factory, and whatever: because that will be each Person's Decision. However, it would Naturally Require a LOT of Slave Labor to do so, which is completely Unnecessary: beCause it is Possible to be Contented with Food and Clothing, even as Jesus Taught. After all, most of the Hard Work will be done by MACHINES at Swanky Fortresses, whereby there will be lots of Free Time to do whatever you Want to do — such as Visit other Beautiful Swanky Fortresses, which could keep you Busy for at least a Billion Years, if you spent 10 Years in each one, trying to Discover all that might be Seen there. After all, there are many People now Living in New York City, who have never Seen the Museum of Natural History, nor even the Trump Tower, much less the thousands of Miles of Streets, and the Insides of each House. Therefore, no one is going to get Bored by the Swanky Fortress System, and *Swanky* Means *First Class Quality* in all Cases within my Literature.

— Chapter 07 —

A Much Better World Without Cars!

07-01 [_] This Subject has already been somewhat Addressed in Chapter 03. However, I want to Emphasize the Facts of the Subject, just to make Sure that no one is left in any Doubt about the EVILS of Capitalism — some of which concern Cars, Gasoline, Pollution, Diseases, Accidents, and Related Subjects, which most People just Ignore — that is, until it Happens to THEM, Personally! Yes, when a Friend or Relative gets Transformed from a Healthy Happy Young Person, into an Instantly Horribly Mangled Bloody Body with Guts Spilled all over everything, and Stink Rising Up into the Nostrils of the Surviving Friends and Relatives, it Suddenly becomes of some Interest to at least Consider another Lifestyle.

07-02 [_] However, when all such Curious People Discover that it is Possible and most Practical to RAISE their Standard of Living by many Times, the Subject becomes of much more Interest.

07-03 [_] O Adolf, if it were Practical to Live without Cars, Vans, Buses, Trucks, Tractors, and all such Things, how come the Communist Chinese or Russians did not Discover it?

07-04 [_] Well, I would say that it simply did not cross their Minds to Build those **"GLORIOUS Swanky Hotels Castles and Fortresses"**: beCause of several Reasons ...

   A-[_] They were Limited by their own Lack of Imaginations, being Restricted by their Pride, which is Blinding to the Mind.

   B-[_] They were Restricted by their Present-day Cities of Confusion, which they did not Want to Abandon, even though that would have been the Wisest Plan: because it would Require a LOT of Wasted Time and Energy to Tear Down and Rebuild all such Cities in the same Places, which are almost always Located along Rivers.

   C-[_] They were not Aware of how much Energy could have been Saved by Building Beautiful Stone Dome Home Complexes for everyone to Live in: beCause of not having any Heating nor Cooling Bills. However, the Russians did not see that as any Waste of Energy: beCause of having an Abundance of Oil and Gas to use; and the Chinese had Visions of Cheap Hydroelectric Power from Dams and Coal-fired Electric Plants.

   D-[_] Moreover, the Chinese People might not think of Swanky Fortresses as being Practical with Rice Patties, which is their Staple Food. However, Rice is a Poor Food, when Compared with Fruits and Vegetables, which are much more Nutritious.

   E-[_] The Russians probably did not want to Build Fortresses that might be "Better-looking" than their present buildings — such as their Painted Wooden / Brick Churches with Onion Domes, such as Saint Basil's Cathedral.

F-[_] Red Jew Bankers did not Want to Solve 5,000 Problems by Building Swanky Fortresses, which might put them Out of Business. For Example, there would be no Need for Fire Insurance: because Rocks do not Catch on Fire.

07-05 [_] O Adolf, it seems to me that if just one Nation got Bold enough to Build just one Swanky Fortress, it would not be long before Multitudes of Swanky Fortresses would Spring Up around the World: beCAUSE of those 5,000+ Good Reasons and Great Advantages for Building them and Living within them.

07-06 [_] Well, one would Think so; but, it is unlikely that the Red Jew News Media would even make a Report about it on TV: beCause, they too would soon Realize the "Grave Danger" of it putting them Out of Business: because they could not Compete with it.

07-07 [_] O Adolf, I would say that all Righteous People would soon Discover those Great Advantages, and thus Decide to Build their own Swanky Fortresses, with or without the Assistance of the New RIGHTEOUS One-World GovernMint.

07-08 [_] Well, they would soon Discover that they could never Afford to Build such Heavy-duty Stone Dome Homes as I Propose, which would have Stone Walls no less than 10 feet THICK, just to Stabilize the Inside Temperatures. Therefore, even with Billions of Dollars, very few Stone Dome Home Complexes could be Built, which would Defeat the Plan. However, with the Assistance of a Righteous One-World GovernMint, which has an Unlimited Amount of New Money, or Credits, to be Earned by Honest Labor, Money is the Least of the Problems.

07-09 [_] O Adolf, I would still want a Car to Haul Home my Groceries, even if I Lived in a Swanky Fortress. Therefore, what are you going to do about that — put me into a Concentration Camp with tens of millions of other Americans?

07-10 [_] No, you would be Welcome to go on Living in some City of Confusion — that is, until the Vast Majority of the People Forsook them, and all of the Grocery Stores were Closed; and then you too would be Forced to Change your Ways of Thinking. After all, your Groceries could be Hauled Home in your own Private Shopping Cart or Wagon, which could be as Big as a Pickup Truck, if you needed it, and be Powered by Pedals: because the Underground Tunnels would be Perfectly Level and Smooth, with no Pot Holes. I would use a Quadruped Cycle, or 4-Wheeled Pedal-powered Wagon, or Pedal-powered Taxi, which could Haul a considerable amount of Groceries for 2 or 3 People, or for an entire Family of 6 or more, depending on the Size of the Machine, which could be Transported by the Electric Subway Train on a Slow Track, over long distances. However, if someone is in a big hurry, he or she could get on a Fast Train Track with a normal Grocery Cart: because all such Railway Cars would be very Spacious, being at least 20 feet wide and 100 feet long with Comfortable Easy Chairs around the inside perimeter of it, which would leave a considerable amount of Space for Wheelchairs, Bicycles, Tricycles, Quadrupeds, and even Electric Cars, if such People Chose to have them. Indeed, there could be a Special Train just for all such Silly People, if they wanted to Work for it. Perhaps you would need an entire Boxcar for Hauling your Groceries Home; but, a normal Shopping Cart would be plenty big enough for me.

— Chapter 08 —

WHO will be Eligible for the DRAFT?

08-01 [_] O Adolf, it is Obvious that most People are NOT going to Voluntarily Join one of your **"Seven Great Armies of Working Soldiers!" (HOW to Provide a Way for Everyone to WORK: so as to Eliminate Poverty, Crimes, Drug Abuses, Prisons and Unnecessary Taxes!)**, Book 015: beCause most of the Young People are now SPOILED by their Soft Lifestyles, whereby the most Work that they might have to do is to empty the Trash into some Street-side Trashcan or Dumpster. Therefore, they know almost nothing about WORKING. Therefore, HOW are you going to get even ONE Swanky Fortress BUILT without a DRAFT?

08-02 [_] Well, I would say that almost all Young People would Cheerfully and Voluntarily Join one of those **"Seven Great Armies of Working Soldiers,"** just to have a Place to Live within a Swanky Palace, as Opposed to Gambling with Capitalism, which has no Guarantee of anything, except more and more DEBTS, beginning with some College Loan Debt, just to get a so-called "good education," so as to Graduate with a "diploma," which is supposed to Qualify such Young People for "Jobs" — such as Flipping Hamburgers in some Greasy Restaurant. However, if they "Fail" in the School of Fools, they might get some Construction Jobs in the Burning Heat of Summer, if those Jobs are not already taken by Poor Mexicans or other "Aliens." Whatever the Case, almost all of them seem to be Unhappy: because the only Thing that they have to Look Forward to is a Pile of Bills to Pay. However, with the System that I Propose, any 12-year-old Person could Volunteer to do some Light Work, and become Moderately Rich within just a few Years, by Working with Adults, who would do the more Difficult and Skilled Labor, who would also become Moderately Rich within just a few Years.

08-03 [_] O Adolf, that Sounds like you would be Breaking Child Labor Laws.

08-04 [_] Well, you must Remember that no such Children would be FORCED to Work: beCause it would only be a Voluntary Arrangement, and only for 3 to 4 Hours per Day: beCause all such Children need to Attend Classes in Schools, just to Learn how to Work Properly. For Example, how many 12-year-old Boys would know HOW to Set Ceramic Tiles on a Wall of a Cistern for Water Storage? How many would know HOW to do All-Mineral Organic Gardening? How many would know HOW to make their own Clothes, HOW to Cook and Can their own Foods, HOW to make their own Furniture, and HOW to Build a Good Stone Wall? Indeed, they would not have to Learn HOW to Do all Kinds of Work; but, at least enough to Survive and Thrive.

08-05 [_] O Adolf, if you had your Way, there would be no Need for Producing Automobiles, Lawnmowers, Weed-eaters, Garden Tillers, nor even Food Blenders: because we would all Revert Back to the Dark Ages, when almost all Families had little Gardens, a Milk Cow, 2 Pigs, and a dozen Chickens for Eggs to Eat. Yes, there are still millions of Poor People who are Living like that. However, I much Prefer to Live on Food Stamps and Welfare. †§‡

08-06 [_] Well, I would say that you Qualify to be DRAFTED into a **Seventh Swanky Army of Working Soldiers,** whereby you can Earn a Good Living without Food Stamps nor Welfare, and end up Living in a Swanky PALACE, which has no Chickens, Hogs, Dogs, Cats, Cattle, nor any other Stinking Beasts: beCause you do not like to Eat Raw Meat, and especially any Stinking Fishes. Indeed, you want someone else — such as some Poor Mexican Slave — to do all of the Dirty Work for you, while you Eat Spicy Cooked Flesh at Fancy Restaurants, without Smelling any Blood nor Guts: beCause you like to Live in a Fantasy World. However, Heinrich Himmler would have you doing the Jobs of those Poor Mexicans, whereby you might Discover the Realities of Life in their World, whereby you might Discover whether or not it is FAIR for them to have to do such Nasty Jobs. For Example, when you get some extra Time, you could take a Trip to Arkansas, whereby you might Visit some of those huge Chicken Houses, where 4 Mexican Slaves are gathering up 90,000 or so Chickens, by Hand, during just one Night, or 22,500 Chickens per Slave: beCause no one has figured out how to do it with Machines. Indeed, each Mexican must bend over and grab the Legs of 5 Chickens in each Hand, and carry them over to a Cage, which holds Exactly 40 Chickens, which are Delivered by 4 of those Poor Overworked Mexican Slaves, who have to Work in a Cloud of Chicken Dust: beCause those Chickens are Aware of what is Happening, and therefore they Try to Escape, whereby they Stir Up a LOT of Dust, and so much so that Visibility is cut down so much that the Chickens cannot See you coming to get them, which makes it easier to Catch them in the Low Light. Meanwhile, your Lungs are Filtering the Air you Breathe, which Causes Emphysema and other Lung Diseases; but, not to Worry: because the Capitalist Job Pays Well at the Rate of about 13 Dollars per Hour, whereby you can Earn 116$ in only 9 Hours, before you Collapse with Exhaustion. Yes, you must Work at Night, when the Chickens are more Sleepy, even in 90 °F Weather, whereby you are Pouring with SWEAT and STINK: beCause hardly anything Smells Worse than a Stinking Chicken House with 30,000 Chickens, with 6-inches or more of Poop on the Ground, and the whole House Covered with Dust on the Rafters and everything within the House. Yes, it is like Visiting HELL, which often Causes new Workers to Vomit within the first Hour of Work: beCause of the STINK and DUST. BUT, the "Good News" is the Fact that no one is FORCED to Do any such Work: beCause it is all VOLUNTARY. Indeed, you are a Poor Mexican, who can always go to Work in the Chicken Plant, processing the Meat, which might Pay a little more than Minimum Wages, whereby you might Afford to Buy some Beans and Tortillas; but, it is hardly enough Money to Prosper on, even if both Husband and Wife are Working in such a Chicken Plant.

08-07 [_] O Adolf, those Bad Working Conditions are only Bad for Mexicans, who are Welcome to go back Home to Mexico, and get similar Capitalist Jobs in Slave-labor Factories over there, if they do not like American Wages, which are 10 Times Better than Mexico Wages: beCause Americans have BILLS to be Paid — such as those Heating and Cooling Bills. For Example, in Arkansas, the Daytime Summer Temperatures are Unbearable with 100% Humidity at 110 °F, which is so HOT as to Melt the Pavement on the Highways. Therefore, one must have Air-conditioning, or else DIE in the HEAT! Likewise, during the Miserable Winters, one must have HEAT, just to keep from Freezing to Death with such High Humidity, which makes your Clothing WET with Sweat, if you do any Hard Work; and then a little Breeze causes you to FREEZE! Therefore, except for a few Months of the Year, Southern United States is like a Living HELL, when Compared with much of Mexico, which is like a Paradise! ‡

08-08 [_] O Adolf, if I were a Poor Mexican, I would LOVE your Master Plan: beCause, if everything is Set Up for LIVING, a Person could easily do enough Work within 3 to 4 Hours to Feed and Clothe himself: beCause there are many Kinds of Fruit Trees in Mexico. For Example, a single Samoan Coconut can easily contain a Quart or Liter of Water, if not 2 Liters; and there are about 20 such Nuts on one Tree, each Month, the Year around. Therefore, if a Family has 4 to 6 such Trees, they could Save thousands of Pesos each Year by not Buying Cokes, nor Beers, whereby they would be much Healthier, Wealthier and Happier. Moreover, a single full-grown Mango Tree might produce 500,000 or more Mangos within 100 Years, which can easily Feed a Family all that they might Want to Eat: beCause they can be Peeled and Pitted and Frozen in Good Condition for 4 to 10 Years in Proper Freezer Boxes. However, not every Year is a Productive Year for all such Fruits. Therefore, it is Good for each Family to have 2 or 3 Mango Trees of Different Varieties, as well as an Avocado Tree, which is Grafted with 3 Kinds: because they Pollinate Better. Otherwise, 3 Different Avocado Trees can be Planted 3 feet apart in a Triangle, whereby their Limbs will Cross over each other, and thus obtain Good Pollination, and enough Fruits to Feed a half-dozen Families all that they might Want. Moreover, there are Lychees, Cherimoyas, Noni Fruits, Rambutans, Yellow Sapotes, Bananas, Papayas, Oranges, and all Kinds of Fruits for making Juices, as well as Figs, and Dates of a hundred Varieties, which can be Grown in Fruit Tree Houses above Covered Highways, even as Master Twain has already Explained in one of his Inspired Books, which has Drawings to Study.

08-09 [_] Well, that is precisely WHY Moses gave Strict Commandments concerning the LAND, which must be Divided among ALL of the People, who must each have a Portion of it for their Gardens, Vineyards, and Orchards, which can be and should be and will be Planted on the ROOFS of their Stone Dome Complexes, if I get in Charge of Things, even if we must Draft 7 Armies of Working Soldiers to get it Done: beCause I am getting SICK of Listening to Sad News Reports about the Extreme Poverty in this World of Woes.

09-10 [_] O Adolf, if you get in Charge of Things around here, it will not be long before all of our Massive Problems will be Solved; and then there will be no more Sensational News Reports, which will make all of us very Unhappy with you: beCause we LOVE those Natural and Manmade DISASTERS! Yes, I can hardly Wait for the next Sad News Report, which Warms Up my Cockles, and makes me Want to go to WAR — except that I have no Idea WHO to Kill FIRST. Yes, I was Thinking that perhaps the Best Place to Begin my Slaughter is in the Local Bank; but, after Studying the Situation, I Discovered that my Financial Problems are NOT Associated with my Local Banker; but, with Chief Red Jew Banksters, who are well Fortified in their Huge Buildings in New Yuck City. Therefore, there is no Way to get to them, let alone get RID of them: beCause they are Surrounded by Armed Guards, and thousands of Policemen. Likewise, I was Thinking that I might make War on the Federal Government, itself; but, after Studying the Situation, I have Concluded that there is no Way that I can Defeat such Well-armed Criminals. Moreover, I was Thinking that I might Assassinate the President; but, after Studying the Situation, I have Concluded that he is just another PUPPET on the Strings of those Puppet Masters in New York City, who Control the Money Supply. Therefore, it is all Extremely Frustrating. Therefore, if you can Muster up an Army for going to War against all such Criminals, I will Gladly Join your Army, and do my Best to get RID of them!

— Chapter 09 —

Adolf's New Army!

09-01 [_] First of all, I want everyone in the World to Understand that I have NO Desire for going to War, even as I had no such Desire in 1938; but, Wicked People are FORCING me into it: beCause of Refusing to DEMAND: **"The Great Worldwide TELEVISED Court HEARING!"** Book 041. Yes, that is the most Practical and Simplistic Way to SOLVE our Massive Problems; but, the Bimbos, Sissies, and Spiritual COWARDS in Washington, District of Criminals, are not at all Interested in anything that might be Reasonable, Logical, Practical, and Useful for Solving our Massive Problems — such as Constructing those **"GLORIOUS Swanky Hotels Castles and Fortresses!" (Beautiful Planned City States for WISE Intelligent Well-Educated People with Common Sense and Good Understanding!)**, Book 019, which will Solve no less than 5,000 Problems! Indeed, none of them are even Willing to Study: **"The Right Design for Living!" (A List of Great Advantages for Building Beautiful Planned City States!)**, Book 012: beCause they did not Propose the Idea. Yes, they Want all of the Glory for themselves for Inventing their own Solutions, which are always very Complicated and Costly, and only a Pretense or Charade of Goodness, which might Help to Relieve the Pains; but, their Solutions never Deal with the ROOT CAUSES for their Ailments, much less TRUE Guaranteed CURES!

09-02 [_] So, O Adolf, it Appears as if you will have to be Elected to be our President, whereby you can Obtain Control of the Military, and become another DICTATOR, just to Straighten us out, huh?

09-03 [_] Well, if it Worked in 1933, I suppose it could Work once again; but, that seems to be a very Painful Way to go about Solving the Problems, since a Voluntary Army of Working Soldiers would not have to Deal with Military Weapons, much less Murdering other Innocent Children. Yes, I Propose that all of my Voluntary Working Soldiers only need to Check the above Box with a Red X, and Sign their Name below above the Dotted Line, even if it is a Fictitious Name, or Nickname, and they will have Joined Forces with us. Yes, by so doing, such a Person will be saying: "I am a Voluntary Member of Adolf Hitler Junior's Army of Working Soldiers." Indeed, that might Sound like a little Joke; but, when 6 Billion People Check their own Boxes in their own Books, and Sign their Names below, it will be a Strong Force to be Reckoned with.

....

Please Check the Box and Sign your Name above in the Blank Space, if you Agree. Thank you.

09-04 [_] Now, here comes the Difficult Part, which is getting other People to Buy a Copy of this Inspired Book, and Persuading them to also Sign their Names, which will Cost less than a Meal of Dog Food or Hog Slop at the Death and Hell Restaurant; but, at the same Time, it will put some Money in my own Bank Account, whereby I might use it Wisely to do some Advertising. Otherwise, you or anyone else could do the Advertising for me, which is fine with me: because I do not Seek Popularity, Fortune, nor Fame. Indeed, I would most Certainly NOT Adopt such a Pen Name as Adolf Hitler, Junior, if I were Seeking any of those Things — much less Capitalize so many Words, which just Naturally Turn Off a LOT of Ignorant People, who have never Studied: **"Justifications for Capitalizations!" (WHY Master Twain Defies the School of Fools by Capitalizing LOVE and HATE!)**, Book 049.

09-05 [_] O Adolf, I must Confess that you are a Genius of Sorts: beCause, if you Manage to Sell 6 Billion Copies of this little Book, you will have about 6 Billion Dollars in your Bank Account, which will be a Fair Amount of Money for one Week's-worth of Work, which seems to be what those Lying Red Jews have been doing all along. Therefore, you must be another one of them, yourself! †§‡

09-06 [_] No, I am an Honest White Jew, who is only Charging a Fair Price for my Inspired Book, while a Lying Red Jew would be Charging no less than TWICE as much Money for it. However, he would never Expect to Sell 6 billion Copies of it; but, I do: because I have an Incredible Amount of FAITH. Indeed, even if People cannot read English, they will be Buying Copies of this Inspired Book, just to get to Sign their Names above the Dotted Line in Verse 09-03: because they are SICK of Living in their Hellish Conditions, when they could all be Living in Beautiful Manmade Paradises! {See www.Amazon.com for: **"The Environmentalists' Paradise!" (HOW almost Everyone could be Living in a Beautiful Manmade Paradise!) By Master Mark Revolutionary Twain, Junior!** Book 035.}

09-07 [_] O Adolf, I Fail to Understand just HOW all such Signatures will have any Positive Effects on the Minds of Politicians in Washington, District of Criminals? Indeed, they will just Ignore you and your Great Multitude of Deceived Followers, as if none of you Existed! †§‡§§

09-08 [_] Are you Kidding? Trust me, there is not another single Person on the Surface of this Earth, who has 6 Billion Followers. Therefore, those Wicked Politicians will hardly be Able to Ignore me and my Followers! In Fact, they will be Begging us to have Mercy on them, and not Boil them in Used Motor Oil in Saint Peter's Plaza, just for being Late at: **"The Great Worldwide TELEVISED Court HEARING!" (That Great Meeting of the Most Intelligent Minds!)**, Book 041.

09-09 [_] God have Mercy, O Adolf! Nobody during all of History ever Sold 6 Billion Copies of any Book, including the Holy Bible! Therefore, HOW in the World do you Expect us to Sell so many Books?

09-10 [_] Well, you are Welcome to KEEP 90 percent of the Net Profits for your own Happiness and Prosperity: because I only Want 10% of the Net Profits for the Construction of **"The Great World TEMPLE of PEACE!" (The Glory of Jerusalem Arises Again!)**, Book 017. Therefore, I am willing to Share my Wealth with whomever has Faith in the Great Truths that I Teach. May all others become Believers during the Future, when they See that Great Temple Springing Up in Jerusalem, right on Top of the Old City!

— Chapter 10 —

Working for Credits!

10-01 [_] Perhaps it does not Sound quite as Exciting as Working for Money; but, since Money, and the Love of Money can Rightly be Blamed for most of the Evils in this World of Woes, it is Time to Rethink the Monetary and Economic System, whereby True Justice can be Obtained for everyone, Worldwide, by the Use of CREDITS.

10-02 [_] So, O Adolf, just Exactly what is your Definition of a "Credit"? Moreover, if I do not already know the Definition, should I Check the above Box with an X?

10-03 [_] Yes, if you do not know the Definition, you should Check that Box: beCause it is like a little Confession, which will Help to Open your Mind for some New Learning, which will be Good for your Soul. First of all, a "Credit" is just a Number in your so-called "Bank Account," which could be nothing more than a Record Book. For Example, let us say that you Set 10 one-foot-square Marble Tiles on a Solid Stone Wall, Properly, you may Receive 10 Credits for it: beCause one Tile is Worth one Credit of Labor, which may be Traded for an Apple, for Example, depending on the Size of it. Otherwise, it could be Traded for whatever is Worth one "Credit," which would have to be Determined by the Supply and Demand for it.

10-04 [_] So, O Adolf, if 100 Million Working Soldiers should get Inspired to Plant 7 Billion Mango Trees, we could Theoretically have "Free" Mangos to Eat, except that someone would have to Harvest those Mangos, which would Require some Labor — say one "Credit" for 10 Mangos: because, while the Tile Setter is Setting just one Marble Tile on the Wall, a Fruit Picker could Harvest 10 Mangos from a Mango Tree, and especially if that Mango Tree were Drooping with Mangos near to the Ground, as they can do and should do and will Do, if those **"Seven Great Armies of Working Soldiers"** go at it Correctly, right?

10-05 [_] That is Correct — the Fruit Trees can be Trained in such a Way as to make Harvesting Fruits rather easy and quick. However, some Fruits will just Naturally be found in the Tops of such Fruit Trees, which will Require the Assistance of Swanky Fruit Picking Machines, which Master Twain has already Explained in other Books for our Enlightenment. (I cannot presently Remember just WHERE such Explanations are Found; but, the Master Index will contain it, when he gets around to making it — that is, if someone else does not get Inspired to make it, who should Notify Master Twain, if they decide to do it.)

10-06 [_] So, O Adolf, WHERE will those Voluntary Working Soldiers be Planting 7 Billion Mango Trees, since they do not Own any Land, which presently Belongs to some Proud Owner, who is not about to Sacrifice his Land to some Extremely Ignorant Voluntary Working Soldiers?

10-07 [_] Well, we Certainly do not Want to call for another World War, just to Obtain some Land to Plant some Fruit Trees on, when there are VAST Wide-open Spaces in Venezuela, for

Example, which would be Ideal Places for Planting 7 Billion Mango Trees — that is, IF there were any Great Demand for all such Frozen Fruits, which can be Transformed into 100% Pure Mango Ice-cream, just by running them through a Meat Grinder, wherever the Boxes of Frozen Mangos have been Shipped to, which, of course, will Require a little more Work, for which some Working Soldiers will have to be given "Credit" in their Bank Accounts.

10-08 [_] O Adolf, suppose I want to Spend my Credits on Candy Bars — will I have your Permission to do so?

10-09 [_] Well, if you want to Rot Out your Precious Teeth, you might be Tempted to Eat Candy Bars; but, I suggest that you Eat Dates, Dried Figs, Yellow Sapotes, Cherimoyas, Bananas, or Mango Ice-cream, which will Satisfy your Natural Hunger for Sweet Things. Yes, the next Time that you get Hungry for something Sweet, just Eat some Raisins with a few Raw Nuts, and Discover for yourself that Natural Foods are Far Superior to anything that Capitalism has to Offer, which does not give a Damn about your Precious Teeth, much less your Good Health: beCause Capitalism is in Business to get as much of your Money as Possible for the Least Amount of Effort, which is HOW certain Rich Red Jews got Billions of People Addicted to Candies, Cokes, Cookies, Cigarette, and all Kinds of Drugs, which you and I should Deny ourselves of: beCause nothing in this World is so Precious as Good Health, which is True Wealth.

10-10 [_] So, O Adolf, do you Sincerely Believe that it might be Possible for a Young Working Soldier to Set enough of those one-foot-square Marble Tiles on the Stone Walls of his own Future House, during one Day, to Pay for all that he and his Family might Eat during one Day, if he only gets one Mango in Exchange for the Credit that he Earned Setting one Tile?

10-11 [_] Well, a Good Tile Setter can Install as many as 40 of those Tiles during 4 Hours, which Means that he could Exchange his Credits for 40 large Mangos, which would be more than he could Eat during one Day, even if he were a PIG. After all, just 2 or 3 such Mangos would Satisfy his Soul for one Meal. Therefore, he might Eat a Total of 12 of them each Day, which would leave plenty for his Family to Eat. Otherwise, he could use his Credits to Buy a Loaf of Whole Wheat Bread, Potatoes, Rice, Broccoli, Cauliflower, Carrots, Beets, or whatever he Wants, which would be for Sale at the Cost of Production, which would be a Minimum Amount: beCause Big Machines would be doing most of the Hard Work. Therefore, he might be able to Trade only 10 Credits for 50 Pounds of Potatoes, unless he had Potatoes in his own Garden for Free, which most Working Soldiers would have — at least during the Season for Growing them — along with many other Kinds of Vegetables, including Sweet Corn, Peppers, Tomatoes, Lettuce, Kale, Collards, and whatever Grows there, which Garden might Require all of 15 Minutes of Work per Day, on Average, which would be a Small Sacrifice for Harvesting TONS of Produce, which could also be Traded for Credits at whatever the Market Value is.

10-12 [_] O Adolf, that Plan might Work Well for some Healthy Young Family; but, what about a Person's Retirement Plan — do you have any Plan for Retirement?

— Chapter 11 —

Adolf's Retirement Plan

11-01 [_] Well, I must Confess that I have not Discovered a Better Retirement Plan than that of Master Mark Revolutionary Twain, Junior, who Addressed that Important Subject in: **"The Swanky Associations of Working Soldiers!" (A Fascinating Collection of Various Kinds of Voluntary Working Soldiers!)**, Book 018, which is rather Ingenious: beCause there is no Need for any Social Insecurity Checks with his Plan, nor will any Old People be Relying on their Poor Children for something to Eat: beCause **the Swanky Association of All-Mineral Organic Gardeners** will be Tithing 10% of their Produce for Feeding all such Old People, Orphans, and Helpless People, who may Eat at the Royal Swanky Buffets, if they want to, along with Elected Officials, Priests, Teachers, Preachers, Architects, Engineers, Authors, Judges, Lawyers, and whomever is Preoccupied with more Important Things than Gardening — even though all People will be Encouraged to have their own Gardens, Vineyards, and Orchards, even if they are Cared for by **the Swanky Association of All-Mineral Organic Gardeners**, who will Naturally be Visiting and Inspecting ALL of the Gardens, just to make Sure that they are in Top Shape: beCause, in Exchange for their Services, all of those Self-disciplined Voluntary Working Soldiers will get to Live in Beautiful Swanky PALACES with Polished Marble Stone Dome Home Complexes with Home-craft Workshops and all of the Wonderful Things that are Described in: **"The Environmentalists' Paradise!" (HOW almost Everyone could be Living in a Beautiful Manmade Paradise!)**, Book 035.

11-02 [_] O Adolf, where do I Sign up? Are you saying that I might only have to do 4 Hours of Common Labor per Day, such as Hoeing Weeds in a Luscious Organic Garden, and get to Live in a GORGEOUS Swanky PALACE!?

11-03 [_] Well, if you People Act Wisely, and put me in Charge of this World, that will Truly be the Case! Guaranteed!

11-04 [_] What if we Refuse to Cooperate with you, O Adolf? Will you Consign us to some Nazi Concentration Camp, or just Cremate us Alive??

11-05 [_] I will run you through a Swanky Meat Grinder, feet first! And then I will Boil you in HOT Used Motor Oil, and at last Feed your Remains to some Hungry HOGS! †§‡

11-06 [_] I sure Hope to God that no one takes that previous Verse Out of Context, O Adolf: because that is very likely going to be their Just Reward, and all for a Lack of Explaining what those Symbols MEAN.

11-07 [_] Well, I Agree with you — that would be their Just Reward. However, to be Perfectly Honest with you, I cannot Imagine any Sane Person on this Earth Refusing to Cooperate with me, seeing that after we get those **"GLORIOUS Swanky Hotels Castles and Fortresses"** finished, they will all be Welcome to Pursue their "Careers," even as Prostitutes and Drug Addicts, if they Want to — if they Willingly CHOOSE to make Fools of themselves. Otherwise, we will DRAFT them into **the Seventh Swanky Army of Working Soldiers**: so that they might Discover what it is Like to Live in a Swanky PALACE!

11-08 [_] O Adolf, your Loving-kindness is far above that of mine: beCause I would have those Rebels WHIPPED with Bull Whips, and sent to Work in Rock Quarries on Minimum Rations of Turnips, Onions, Garlic, Recycled Sewage Water, and whatever might be Found in Dumpsters! §

11-09 [_] Now, Pray Tell, WHY would you Want to be so Mean to the Teenage Children, who have been Depressed for so long with Capitalist Lies, many of whom have already Committed Suicide? Why not be Patient with them? After all, there is no BIG Hurry to get those Fortresses Built, if we are Relying on Climate Changes to WHIP their Asses: beCause Dramatic Things could Happen if the Oceans should Suddenly RISE by 10 Meters! Yes, that is a Possibility, which no one is Prepared for, including myself: beCause it would be an Extremely Unusual Thing to Happen. However, the SUNLIGHT could Suddenly become HOTTER, whereby the Ice would Suddenly MELT, and then Lungdung, England, and New Yuck City would be Under the Water! Yes, Moscow, Hong Kong, Sydney, Seattle, Los Angeles, Miami, Rio de Janeiro and many Major Cities around the World would be DROWNED OUT! Therefore, this is Serious Business that we are Addressing, and not some Childish Nonsense. Yes, you will also Capitalize Serious and Business when it Happens, O Drunken Ducks!

11-10 [_] O Adolf, if this were not a very Serious Book, I would be Laughing: beCause you are a Good Comedian, and probably do not even Realize it. After all, there is no Way on this Earth that Antarctica is going to SUDDENLY MELT! Are you not Aware that the Ice down their is 3 Miles THICK?

— Chapter 12 —

Scientists have been WRong Before!

12-01 [_] O Adolf Junior, the Worst Mistake that Adolf Hitler made during World War 2, was Listening to his Weather Prognosticators, who Falsely Predicted that it would be a MILD Winter in Russia, when the Germans would Attack, which turned out to be one of the Worst Winters in Russian History! Yes, Adolf Senior sent his Troops over there without any Winter Clothing on, as if his Weather Prognosticators were Holy Prophets, and 100% Correct: beCause he Trusted them, when he should have gone to his Knees in Prayer to Almighty God, who would have Naturally Warned him that it was going to be a very BAD Winter. Yes, any Honest Priest or Pastor of any Church would have known that, if he had only Consulted them; but, behold, he was too Proud and Puffed Up with "Scientific Nonsense," just like those Dimwitcrats and Reprobates in Washington, who have no Idea what a single Day will bring forth, let alone a whole Year!

12-02 [_] Well, O Doctor Reverend Billy Graham, I must Agree with you about all of that. Indeed, it was a Case where Adolf Senior should have been Extremely Cautious with such a Military Maneuver: beCause his entire War Depending on Winning in Russia. Therefore, he should have Ordered his Troops to Retreat, until he could get them Properly Prepared for such a War. But, better yet, he should not have Attacked Russia, until he was Well-prepared for it. However, he Calculated that if he put it Off for another Year, the Russians would be too well Armed, whereby he might be Defeated by them, anyway. Therefore, it was a Great Gamble, which he Lost. However, in my Case, I have all my "Spiritual Weapons" Lined Up and Ready for Battle against whomever might Oppose me, who only have their Weak Rubber Swords to Fight with, who most likely never even Heard of the Sharp Sword of Divine Truths that I Wield, which is far more Powerful than anything a Dimwitcrat or Reprobate might have on his Side.

12-03 [_] O Adolf Junior, if your "Father" had been Wise, he would have Won the Hearts and Minds of the Russians, first, with his Sword of Truths. After all, more than 300,000 Russians Joined Forces with him when he did Attack: because they Hated that Wicked Joseph Stalin, who had already Murdered Millions of Innocent Russians, which was a Major Reason WHY Adolf Hitler wanted to get RID of him. However, American Leaders Deceived themselves, and Joined the Wrong Army, unto their own Great Shame: beCause of being Afraid that your Father might Attack them next, if he Defeated the Russians, which was a Likely Thing to Happen: because the Russians were not very Good Warriors, seeing that they Lost some 22 Million Soldiers, while the Germans lost less than a Million to the Russians. However, being a Small Nation, it was a Fruitless Goal: because there was no Way that the Germans could have Managed all of the People in the whole World, even if they had Won the War, Worldwide: beCause they could only Spread themselves Out just so Thin, before being Overcome by their Enemies, if those Enemies were Determined to Defeat them. Indeed, Americans might Imagine that they Presently Dominate the whole World, just beCause of their Military Might; but, if all Nations Turned Against Americans, they would easily be Defeated: beCause of being far Outnumbered. Indeed, the Russians and Chinese could Defeat the United States, just by themselves. †§‡

12-04 [_] Well, in an Atomic Age like this, whomever Strikes First would be the Victor, if they had everything Lined Up Properly, which they could do; but, of course, Americans would Retaliate, and leave many Cities in Ashes, even if the People did Survive: beCause of being in Underground Bunkers, Subways, and in Secret Places. After all, Americans hardly have any Protection from such Bombs, while the Russians and Chinese have lots of Protection, and Good Food Supplies. Therefore, you could Honestly say that Americans are Ignorant Fools for leaving themselves so Vulnerable to Nuclear Attacks, which could be Over with in less than one Hour. Yes, *"in One Hour her Destruction will Come,"* just as *the Book of Revelation* Prophesies: beCause she is in Word and in Deed *"the Whore of all of the Earth,"* who Specializes in Drugs, which has been her Primary Business ever since the Founding Fathers Fought the Revolutionary War, which began over some Tea, which was just another Drug, even though less Addictive than Coffee, Cokes, Tobacco and Alcohol, which was George Washington's Favorite Commodities for Sale, who was another Drug Addict, which can be Proven in a Courtroom. †§‡

12-05 [_] O Adolf, I must Disagree with you about that. George Washington was a True Christian, who read his Bible every Day, and Prayed to God every Morning and Night: because he was a God-fearing Man with a Bald Head and False Teeth: beCause he also Trusted in "Science" and Medical Doctors, who Bled him to Death: beCause Bleeding was their Customary Treatment at that Time for Insanity and almost anything you might Name: beCause most of those Ignorant People Ignored the Great Truths in the *Bible* about Fasting and Praying, which is Nature's One and ONLY Cure for all Wild Animals, which can be, should be, and must be Proven at: **"The Great Worldwide TELEVISED Court HEARING,"** just to get the Record Straight about those Phony Medical Doctors. {See www.Amazon.com for: **"Did God or Satan Ordain Medical Doctors??" (Ask Huck Finn and/or Nigger Jim: because neither Tom Sawyer nor Judge Thatcher would Know!)**, Book 022.}

12-06 [_] Well, you must Remember that if you Disagree with me about any certain Subject, you are Welcome to Address your Disagreement to: **"FREEDUM uv SPEECH!" (U Speshoul Maguzeen uv Onust Upinyunz!)**, Book 030.

12-07 [_] O Adolf, I have no Idea HOW to make Contact with you, whereby I might Address any certain Subject with my Honest Opinion.

12-08 [_] Well, there is a Way to Contact me with a Personal E-mail Letter, if you can Find my Address, which is Hidden in one of the Inspired Books by Master Mark Revolutionary Twain, Junior.

12-09 [_] O Adolf, WHY would he Hide his Mailing Address?

12-10 [_] Well, you might not Believe it, even as many People do not; but, Master Twain is at the Head of the List of the Most Wanted Americans, Dead or Alive: beCause he is a Great Threat to the Evil Capitalist Empire. Otherwise, that Wicked Anti-Christ Cover-up False Federal Government might Reward him with a Social Security Check, just for being a Good Boy, you might say: because he has no Police Record, nor any other Criminal Record. In other Words, he is as Good as Americans come, who started out as a Montana Cowboy, Meat Wrapper, Soldier, Carpenter, Organic Gardener, Stone Mason, Tile Setter, Theologian, Author, Printer, Bookbinder, Book Publisher, and Inventor of many Wonderful Things. †§‡

— Chapter 13 —

Will Adolf Hitler Junior Commit Suicide?

13-01 [_] Well, if someone tells you that I have Committed Suicide, you can be Sure that they are WRong about that: beCause I am the Healthiest Happiest Person that I know of at my Age, which is a Considerable Age, when you Consider the Fact that I should have Worked myself to Death, by now. For Example, my Brother and I moved more than 13,000,000 Pounds during 7 Years, by Hand, in order to Build our Rock Houses, which have Roofs that are 3 to 6 feet thick, being mostly Rough Rocks and Concrete. However, we did have some Help on that Project, as with most of our Projects, even though we did at least 80% of the Work in all Cases, including the Construction of our Retirement Home, which has no less than 50 Dump-truckloads of Washed Gravel in it, which my Brother and I had to Wash with a small Concrete Mixer: beCause there was MUD on the Gravel, which would Naturally not Stick very well to Cement / Concrete, which Requires CLEAN Sand and Gravel. Once again, we can Blame Capitalism for that Sin: beCause Unwashed Gravel almost Guarantees the Concrete "to go to Hell," as my Brother would say: beCause of the Fact that Mud does not Stick in Concrete very well. Moreover, such Unwashed Gravel is still being used, Legally, by Concrete Companies: beCause it is "Good for business," they say, even as it is "Good for Business" for Capitalists to make Cheap Cars, which are Designed to Break Down at about the same Time the Guarantees Expire, which is True of most Capitalist Trash that fills up "landfills," which plan will be Abandoned during the Future, when I get into Control, if God is Willing, and I perceive that he is Willing; but, the Capitalist Hogs are not Willing: beCause they are Afraid of being put Out of Business! ‡

13-02 [_] O Adolf, I have seen a few of those "landfills," and I must Confess that it is a Great Shame on Americans, who should have to Pitch their Tents in all such Landfills, until they Change their Minds, if they do not Agree with me about that. In Fact, I will be Happy to take Charge of your Gestapo SS Troops, just to Help them to Pitch their Tents in those Stinking Landfills, if they do not Quickly Agree with you and me, and Check the above Box.

13-03 [_] Well, Thank you for your Offer, since it is rather Generous of you; but, I Seriously Doubt that anyone will be Brave enough to Stand Up at **"The Great Worldwide TELEVISED Court HEARING,"** and say that they LOVE those Landfills, and that they are not a Shame on us to have them, and Plans for making millions more of them, Worldwide. Indeed, the First Person who does Attempt to Defend such Trash Dumps will have to Live in them for the Remainder of his or her Life, just for Punishment! Therefore, Spread the WARNING! †§‡

13-04 [_] O Adolf, I recently took a Cruise Ship across the Ocean, and stayed on Deck for much of the way, and noticed that the Ocean was Littered with Trash for as far as my Eyes could See! In Fact, there was not so much as one Clean Mile of Water on the entire Trip. Therefore, I am now Wondering just Exactly what your Plans might be for Cleaning up those Oceans, Lakes, Rivers, and Polluted Wells? After all, if we are going to Elect a DICTATOR, we might as well get something Worthwhile for our Effort!

13-05 [_] Well, those Oceans will have to be Cleaned Up by those Capitalist Pigs who Produced all of that Trash. For Example, when we find a Used Coke Can floating around on the Sea, the Company that Sold the Can or Bottle will be Responsible for Cleaning Up all of those Cans in all of the Oceans, Seas, Lakes, Rivers, and wherever they are Discovered. Otherwise, we, the People, will put them Out of Business by Refusing to Buy any more of their Trash. †§‡

13-06 [_] O Adolf, are you not being a little too Harsh on all such Capitalist Companies, who could not be Legally Responsible for what their Customers might Do with their Used Bottles.

13-07 [_] Well, they Failed to put any Labels on their Containers, stating so, nor Warning their Customers of the Dangers of Disposing of all such Trash, Illegally — such as Throwing Trash into the Oceans. Therefore, I would say that they are Responsible from now on to get their Labels Correct, and to also Warn their Potential Customers of the Dangers in Consuming all such Harmful Chemicals and Poisons: beCause, if they do not get their Acts Together by the Time that I am Elected to be the Dictator, they will Wish to God that they had never been Born! Yes, we will send the Gestapo SS after them, and Round them up for Trials, at which Time they will be Found GUILTY as Charged, beginning with those Red Jews who Control the Advertising of all such Trash and Poisons. For Example, how many Chief Executives at NBC, ABC, CBS, and other Networks PAID for the Medical Care of the Capitalist Victims of Smoking and Chewing Tobacco? Answer: NONE. Indeed, they Totally Skipped Out on all Responsibilities for Advertising their Lies and Deceptions. Therefore, they will either Cooperate with us, or we will put all of them OUT of Business! Moreover, they can Begin their Cooperation right now, by Advertising this Good Book for Sale, unless they Want to Publish it, Worldwide, in all Major Languages, Free of Charge, which they are Welcome to Do, which they can send to every Mailbox in the World; and then we will Forgive them for all of the Years of Advertising Lies, Drugs, Alcoholic Beverages, Stinking Noisy Cars, Lawnmowers, Weed-eaters, Motorcycles, 4-Wheelers, Snow Blowers, Garden Tillers, and whatever. ‡

13-08 [_] O Adolf, are you not being a little too HARSH on those Capitalist HOGS? Are you Sure that they will not have you ASSASSINATED?

13-09 [_] No, they will NOT have me Assassinated: beCause that would be like Signing their own Death Warrants: beCause the Masses of Deprived People LOVE me, even as they should: beCause, if they Love and OBEY me, they will all get to Live in Beautiful Swanky PALACES! Therefore, it is not Wise of anyone to Imagine that getting Rid of me is a Good Idea: beCause I am the only Person in the World who has the WISDOM of King Solomon, which you will never Doubt, if you just Study: **"Thu Nq MAGNUFIID Verzhun uv Thu PROVERBZ uv KING SOLUMUN in Plaan Ingglish!" (The Understandable Version of the Famous Proverbs of King Solomon in Plain English!)**, Book 028, which is a Companion Book of: **"ECCLESIASTES UNCOVERED!" (The New MAGNIFIED Version of Ecclesiastes and the Song of Solomon in Plain English!)**, Book 034, which will Fully Persuade any Intelligent Person on this Earth that I am in Fact the Reincarnation of King Solomon!

13-10 [_] So, O Adolf, are you Confessing that you are NOT the Reincarnation of Adolf Hitler? Are you just another LIAR, or what??

— Chapter 14 —

The Conclusion

14-01 [_] Well, as the Apostle wrote in *Romans 3:4, "Let God be True; but, every Man a Liar,"* which does Sound a bit Strange — as if Paul were Suggesting that every Man should be a Liar: because only God could be True. However, he was probably Trying to say: *"Let God be True to his own Words, even if every Man is found to be a Liar, even as it is written, so that you, O God, might be Justified by your Words, and thus Prevail when anyone Seeks to Judge you."* — NMV.

14-02 [_] O Adolf, your other Ridiculous Books Claim that you are the Reincarnation of Mark Twain, himself. Therefore, is there any Truth in that?

14-03 [_] Well, that Remains to be Proven in God's Courtroom, which could be True, even though I never did Like the Idea: beCause Mark Twain (Samuel Langhorne Clemens) was not Exactly the Best of Characters who ever Lived; but, like he wrote in *"The Adventures of Tom Sawyer,"* it is mostly a True Story, which is probably about as Accurate as most of the *Bible,* I might add: beCause that is how he Felt about it. (See *"Letters from the Earth"* for the Proof.) Yes, after more than 60 Years of Bible Study, I have come to the Conclusion that much of it is Fictitious, being a Concoction of Lying Red Jews for the most Part, even though I will Confess that much of it does read like a True Story, even from *Genesis* onward, up to the Noah Story, which no Person with a Sound Mind could Accept as being 100% True, or even 50% True: beCause of many Reasons that I have already Pointed Out in: **"What is WRong with those Professing Christians?" (A Self-Examination of the Heart of the Body of Good Government!)**, Book 002, which lays out the Cold Hard Facts of the Matter for any Honest Person to Study.

14-04 [_] O Adolf, when you become the Chief Dictator of the Whole World, do you Want us to call you "Adolf," "Master Twain," or what? Indeed, if I Understand it Correctly, you also have other Pen Names, which will be Disclosed later on.

14-05 [_] Well, to be Perfectly Honest with you, I would Prefer ... well, I had best not say, as yet: beCause that particular Name does not set Well with Professing "Christians," who would just Naturally Assume that I must be the Anti-Christ, himself; but, there is Absolutely NO Truth in that: beCause I have nothing Against Jesus Christ, at all, whom I have Seen Face to Face, who Sealed me with his own Personal Seal on my Forehead and in the Palm of my Right Hand. Therefore, until he takes it away, you might say that I am SEALED as one of his True Servants.

14-06 [_] O Adolf, do you also Sincerely Believe that Adolf Hitler was Sealed by God to do whatever he did?

14-07 [_] Well, I Sincerely Believe that all of the Leaders of this World have been Ordained by SATAN, and NOT by God: beCause "God" is "All that is Good," who has left this World in

Charge of Satan, the Devil, who is "All that is Evil." Therefore, I would say that my New MAGNIFIED Version of Romans 13 is much more Accurate, which you can Discover in one of Master Twain's Inspired Books. (It could be in **"What is WRong with those Professing Christians?"** — but, I cannot Rightly Remember. I do Desperately Need that Master Index finished: so that I might make more Accurate References.)

14-08 [_] O Adolf, I had it in my Mind that Master Twain was fixing to Raise Up some Woolly Mammoth Elephants from his own Garden, and also get some Rough Rocks Transformed into Pure Gold; but, I guess that was all some more LIES, huh?

14-09 [_] Well, I have not altogether given up on that Idea. After all, with the Help of God, all Good Things are Possible. The Great Question is this: **"Would it turn out to be a Good Act, or an Evil Act, seeing that it could be Misunderstood?"** Indeed, Ignorant People could begin to Imagine that they should be Worshiping ME, as if I were GOD! Yes, many of them would say that I must be Jesus Christ, himself, when I have never Said any such thing, nor have I ever Written it. Moreover, I am not at all Tempted to Vainly Imagine that I am in Fact, Jesus Christ, himself: because of several Reasons, which I will not now bother you with; but, you can Trust me, when I say that I am far from being Qualified for any Worship of any Kind. However, that is not to say that I should not be Greatly Respected for all of the Great Truths and Wisdom that God has Revealed to me, which can easily be Discovered within my Inspired Books, which are most Definitely Inspired by GOD, which can be Proven in a Courtroom: beCause they Draw all People Closer to God, even if only in small Degrees: beCause of the Multitude of Provable Truths within them.

14-10 [_] O Adolf, WHY are there only 10 Verses in each Chapter of many of your Inspired Books? Is that some Signature Message that all Diligent Readers should Understand, whereby your Books can be Identified as being Different than those of any other Author on this Earth? Indeed, it Worries me that all such Chapters might have 99 Verses during the Future, which would Explain WHY the Present Chapters go up to Verse 10, whereby Computers can keep Track of them in a Proper Way, even if there are 99 Verses. Moreover, when we all get to Heaven, I do Hope to God that I find the Time to Study ALL of your 300+ Inspired Books, which are likely to be 500+ by the Time that you Finish Writing them! In Fact, if you Live for another 100 Years, there might be a thousand or more of them, which would Certainly Set a World Record that no one else could ever Match, seeing that not even Sir William Shakespeare could Measure Up to such Endless Nonsense! †§‡

— Chapter 15 —

Supplemental Thoughts

15-01 [_] Well, there was a Time, not long ago, when I was Thinking about Writing *My Struggle / Mein Kamph* in another 720-page Book, just to keep the Bloodhounds at Bay; but, then I got to Considering the Fact that most People are Extremely Poor, and could never Afford to Buy such a large Book, which would be about 75$; and therefore, I said to myself: "If they Buy this little Book for only 6$, and do their Best to Help me to Publish it all around the World, I can provide all of my other Inspired Books for FREE, on the Internet, if I am Elected to be the DICTATOR." Therefore, I still Believe that such a Plan is a Good Idea: beCause I can also Publish the Original Book about the Loathsome Burdens of the Independent Jackasses, which is actually Better than this Book in many Ways; but, not for whatever Reason that God Wanted it this Way, which will Prove to be Best in the End — and especially if it "Jump Starts" all of my Inspired Books, all of which are Exceptionally Good, in my Honest Opinion. In Fact, if they were not so, I would not Publish them.

15-02 [_] O Adolf, I would LOVE to read ALL of your Inspired Books, no matter what your Pen Names might be: beCause I am Sure that I could Discover Great Truths within them, which cannot be Found in any other Books. For Example, this Inspired Book Reveals HOW to Clean Up those Oceans, Seas, Lakes, Rivers, and Landfills: so that the Earth might be a Decent Place for Jesus Christ to Return to. After all, it is Doubtful that he will Return to such a Polluted World as this, until it is Cleaned Up, which is OUR Responsibility.

15-03 [_] Well, as the Man with the Spirit of Elijah, I must Agree with you — it MUST be Cleaned Up, and Straightened Out before his Second Coming. Therefore, if you are a Professing "Christian," you will do your Ever-loving Best to Assist me to get into Control of this World, by DEMANDING: **"The Great Worldwide TELEVISED Court HEARING!"** Book 041. Yes, it might seem to be a bit Spooky; but, this is the End of this Age, and we are now at a Crossroads, you might say, whereby we must Decide to go RIIT or Left or Straight Ahead into HELL!

15-04 [_] O Adolf, I will Confess one Thing, and that is the Fact that IF this Book is Inspired by Yohoovu God, he Certainly has a Strange Sense of HUMOR: beCause there is really nothing very Funny about it, whereas Master Twain is FULL of Humor, whose Inspired Books are much more Enjoyable than this one. However, if this is what it Requires to "Jump Start" all of your Books into the Marketplace, then so be it. Yes, I am Willing to Play along with it: beCause I am FED UP with those Wicked Satanic Politicians in the District of Criminals, in Washington, who most Definitely need to be taken to COURT, and Charged with TREASON, just for Ignoring the Evil Events of September 11th, 2001, which could not have Possibly been "Pulled Off" by Arabian Hijackers, who had ZERO Training for doing what they Allegedly did, which not even a Professional Pilot could have done without the Stress of Hijacking an Airplane, which any Honest Pilot will Freely Confess, without being Water Boarded. Therefore, those SINators and CONgressmen should have to Prove their "Conspiracy Theories" to be True: beCause no

Professional People will Support their False Claims, GUARANTEED! {See www.AE911TRUTH.org for the Proof, as well as YouTube Videos for Dr. Judy Wood and *Experts Speak Out,* which Debunk the Official False Cover-up Reports.}

15-05 [_] Well, that is what I have been "Preaching" for no less than 10 Years.

15-06 [_] O Adolf, suppose you get your Way, will you Keep your Promises?

15-07 [_] Well, even *my* Mind is Subject to Change: beCause of Learning New Information. However, my Promises concerning **that Great Meeting of the Most Intelligent Minds** is as Steadfast as the Rock of Gibraltar! Yes, that is the KEY to Solving ALL of our Massive Problems, Worldwide.

15-08 [_] O Adolf, if you do get Assassinated, somehow, or just get Run Over by a Bus when going Shopping, I will Feel Extremely Depressed: beCause you Offer more Hope than we have ever Heard before, even from Jesus Christ, himself.

15-09 [_] Well, you must Remember that it was his Inspired Words that Inspired me to Write my Inspired Books. Therefore, all Glory and Honor must go to him, alone, whether or not I Live or Die, which is really up to God to Decide: because he has Saved my Life many Times, even in Hateful Wars. For Example, a Grenade went off just 4 feet from my Head in Vietnam, and I never got a Scratch, nor did any of the 16 Men who Obeyed me, which I have Revealed in another Good Book.

15-10 [_] O Adolf, I can hardly Wait to read all about it! Indeed, you have Lived a very Remarkable Life, I must Confess, and likely Hold several World Records — one of which is to Write an Inspired Book like this in less than one Week! Yes, that is AMAZING! After all, I could not do it in a whole Month, and I am also an Author. Yes, I will Challenge myself to do something similar, just to Prove it to myself. Therefore, if you Believe in LUCK, please Wish to me some Luck: beCause I have been writing uninspired books for many years, and none of them Compare with this one, which might easily Sell a Million Copies, if not 6 Billion!

The Loathsome Burdens of the Independent Jackasses!

"Adolf Hitler, Junior," is much more Cunning than his "Father," who Lost the Great World War; but, not this Time around: beCause his "Son" has Brand New Ideas in his Mind, which are quite Dumbfounding, we must Confess with a Capital D and C, which you can Discover for less than the Price of another Hamburger, French Fries and a Coke, which will Greatly Satisfy the Belly of your Mind, if you Chew it Thoroughly with a Capital T, which the Doctor Good Health Strongly Recommends. Yes, the Apostle James summed it up in a single Verse: *"Behold, what a Great Matter a Little Fire can Kindle!"* And is this little book not much more Flammable than anything that we have ever Seen? Yes, it calls for: **"Seven Great Armies of Working Soldiers!"** — which, we must Confess, sounds a whole lot Better than Nazi Prison Camps and War Machines!